The
1906–1910
Cubs Dynasty

THE
1906–1910
CUBS DYNASTY

Rowdy Times and Rugged Men in Cutthroat Chicago

GARY D. SANTELLA

THE
History
PRESS

Published by The History Press
Charleston, SC
www.historypress.com

First published 2024

Manufactured in the United States

ISBN 9781467156790

Library of Congress Control Number: 2023950480

To Mary Kay

CONTENTS

ACKNOWLEDGEMENTS

I'd like to thank my siblings Glenn and Gloria for taking the time to read my manuscript and provide me with their helpful comments and edits. A special thanks to my brother Andrew, who allowed me on several occasions to tap into his considerable experience in the literary world and offered helpful suggestions.

Thanks also to my friends Marell and Cliff Kowalski, as well as my friend Dr. Edward Rossini, all of whom continued to show interest in this project year after year until it was finally completed. I'd also like to acknowledge the late Claude Ohanesian, whose contagious enthusiasm for the project—despite being a rabid St. Louis Cardinals fan—inspired me to keep going. I only wish that he had lived long enough to see the work completed.

I am grateful for the professionalism of Ben Gibson, Rick Delaney and Hilary Parrish at The History Press, all of whom capably and patiently guided me through the editing and publication process.

I appreciate the assistance I received from the staff and reference librarians at the Chicago History Museum, most notably Elizabeth McKinley, Maggie Cusick, Angela Hoover and Natalie Sinclair. They helped me to access and review numerous articles and vintage photos from early 1900s Chicago.

I'd like to thank my teachers at Saint Patrick High School in Chicago. Decades ago, they taught me the joy of reading and learning. I also want to thank the current teachers there, who carry on their important work for today's students.

I look forward to passing down this book—and thus a little part of myself—to my children, Katie, Caroline and Colleen, as a token of all the love and pride I feel for each of them.

Most important, thanks to Mary Kay, for her helpful input in this project and for everything else. I can always count on her for her never-ending support, advice and love. She is truly amazing!

INTRODUCTION

In the midst of winter, I found there was, within me, an invincible summer.
—Albert Camus

When Cubs third baseman Kris Bryant fielded a slowly hit grounder, smiled and threw to first baseman Anthony Rizzo to seal the 2016 World Series championship, Cubs Nation burst into a seismic celebration. In quiet Chicago neighborhoods, the sound of firecrackers abruptly pierced the night. In the Wrigleyville area, streets were quickly closed in deference to revelers, whose elation could no longer be contained within the bounds of their local drinking establishments. Over the next few days, fans from all around the world would scribble with chalk on the brick outer walls of Wrigley Field to proclaim their devotion to the Cubs, and millions of fans would line the streets to pay homage to their idols during the Cubs' massive victory parade.

Not for 108 years had there been cause for a Cubs World Series celebration. Back then, however, Cubs fans had even more to celebrate than a solitary pennant and World Series championship. The 1906–10 Cubs were a major league "dynasty." They would win four National League pennants (1906, 1907, 1908 and 1910) and two World Series titles (1907 and 1908) in just five seasons.

During that first decade of the twentieth century, a common trait that defined both the people of the city of Chicago and the Cubs was "toughness"—physical toughness and, more productively, toughness of character.

Widespread streetfighting by brawlers and thugs, often carrying billy clubs and blackjacks, epitomized the city's physical toughness. Ordinary citizens often brandished pistols in public. Acts of rowdiness, fisticuffs and violence were so commonplace that the clenched fist would have been a fitting emblem for the city. A half century later, radio comedian Fred Allen joked, "Things are so tough in Chicago that at Easter time, for bunnies the little kids use porcupines." That quote would have been just as applicable for early twentieth-century Chicago.

If widespread streetfighting and other violence were not enough, vice and blatant political corruption pervaded the city. Nowhere was this more prevalent than in Chicago's First Ward, where "protection payments," bribes and other payoffs demanded by its two corrupt aldermen, John "Bathhouse" Coughlin and Michael "Hinky Dink" Kenna, turned the ward into their personal gold mine. (From 1897 through 1923, Chicago's wards each had two aldermen. The First Ward's two aldermen were Coughlin and Kenna. It has been jokingly suggested that two aldermen were needed because there was simply too much graft for one alderman to handle.)

The city's toughness of character was best embodied by its proactive and resilient civic and business leaders, who were willing to think boldly, act fearlessly, take risks, innovate and overcome adversity after the Great Fire of 1871. They created new industries, built skyscrapers, hosted a cutting-edge World's Fair and much more. All the while, the city grew at an astonishing rate.

The Chicago Cubs back then were no strangers to toughness, either. Like the city they played for, they exhibited both physical toughness and toughness of character. No one was more physically tough than their husky, fearless player-manager and "Peerless Leader," Frank Chance, who skirmished with opposing players, his own teammates and even spectators. Other Cubs players bickered and brawled with the opposition and one another, on the field and in the locker room. Cubs second baseman Johnny Evers and shortstop Joe Tinker fought with and hated each other. Despite working together every game, they didn't speak to one another for years. Chance developed a loathing for the team's owner, and star catcher John Kling clashed with management over money and left the team for a year to play professional billiards.

Like their city, the Cubs also displayed toughness of character. They played fearlessly, imaginatively, resiliently and with justified confidence. Again, it was Chance, the Peerless Leader, who set the example, especially while facing adversity. With both kinds of toughness buttressing the exceptional talent on their roster, the Cubs dominated the National League from 1906 to 1910, won two world championships and shared with their fans a wild ride in the process.

////

To understand in context the story of that remarkable early twentieth-century Cubs team, and to grasp how its toughness embodied its city at the time, let's gain some perspective by going back to the respective beginnings of both the City of Chicago and the Chicago Cubs.

PART I

CHICAGO AND BASEBALL
BEFORE THE FIRE

Chapter 1

THE BIRTH OF CHICAGO

I think that's how Chicago got started. A bunch of people in New York said,
"Gee, I'm enjoying the crime and the poverty, but it just isn't cold enough.
Let's go west."
—Richard Jeni

Perhaps no spot in Chicago better exemplifies the city's stunning transformation from its initial beginnings to today than the location on the Chicago River near Lake Michigan where the ultra-modern Michigan Avenue Apple store stands. At that location in 1794, a Black fur trader from the Caribbean named Jean-Baptiste Pointe du Sable established an isolated trading post. It is anyone's guess why du Sable chose to settle there. Perhaps he needed some quiet time. Maybe he had a keen eye for real estate and was an early adherent of the mantra "location, location, location." Then again, it is also possible that his wife, a member of the local Potawatomi tribe, insisted that he maintain their home near the in-laws and that the dutiful husband did what he was told.

In any event, du Sable became Chicago's first non-native permanent resident, and soon a small trading settlement was established there. In 1803, the U.S. government built Fort Dearborn to protect the settlement.

Shortly after the War of 1812 began, the British, Canadians and their Native American allies, working together, captured Fort Mackinac in northern Michigan. The U.S. Army, fearing the same fate for Fort Dearborn, ordered its garrison to evacuate and retreat to Fort Wayne. The 148 soldiers and residents of Fort Dearborn and its settlement, including women and children, left the fort and headed south and east for Fort Wayne, located in present-day Indiana.[1]

Anecdotally, the soldiers and settlers had agreed to provide the local Native American tribe, the Potawatomi, with weapons in exchange for safe passage, but there is speculation that the soldiers and settlers may have reneged on the deal. In any event, after traveling only a mile or two south to a location somewhere between today's Roosevelt Road and Eighteenth Street, the evacuating soldiers and settlers were brutally attacked by five hundred Potawatomi. In a matter of minutes, many of the outmanned soldiers and settlers were massacred, including children. Others were taken prisoner.[2]

The tragedy has come to be known as the "Fort Dearborn Massacre," and the event is memorialized by the first of the four red stars on the flag of the City of Chicago. Unfortunately, the Fort Dearborn Massacre marked the beginning of a never-ending chain of fighting, violence and bloodshed that would haunt Chicagoans to the present day.

In 1816, a new Fort Dearborn was established at the same location, as was a new settlement. In 1837, the settlement was incorporated as the City of Chicago. The new city became a destination for many newcomers drawn by the economic opportunities afforded by its ideal location near Lake Michigan and in the center of the continent. That ideal location precipitated Chicago's becoming a major Great Lakes shipping port and rail transportation center.[3]

By 1860, Chicago's population was more than one hundred thousand, and the city had taken on such a national stature that it was chosen to host the inaugural Republican National Convention, which would nominate Illinois' Abraham Lincoln as its candidate for the U.S. presidency.

By 1870, the city's population had exploded to nearly three hundred thousand.[4] Entrepreneurs and industrialists built manufacturing and industrial plants. Marshall Field built a store, and Potter Palmer built a hotel. The population continued to grow. The city's growth was so astounding that, for decades during the nineteenth century, Chicago was the fastest-growing city in the world.

Chapter 2

THE BIRTH OF CHICAGO BASEBALL

Baseball…the very symbol, the outward and visible expression of the drive and push and rush and struggle of the raging, tearing, booming 19th Century.
—Mark Twain

In 1870, a Chicago ball club called the "White Stockings"—the predecessor to today's Cubs—was organized. (Late in the nineteenth century and into the very early twentieth century, the White Stockings dropped their moniker in favor of a string of other names, eventually becoming known as the "Cubs." In the early 1900s, the upstart American League entry from the South Side would then appropriate for itself a variation of the old White Stockings moniker and would be known as the "White Sox.")

In its first season, on September 7, 1870, the White Stockings took on the mighty Cincinnati Red Stockings in Cincinnati, or "Porkopolis," as it was sarcastically referred to by Chicago news reporters in reference to the prominence of the pork-packing industry there.[5]

The year before, in 1869, the Red Stockings had become the first professional baseball team and won all fifty-seven of their games in their first season.[6] They were considered invincible. As the September 7 game day drew near, anticipation in Chicago intensified. In the meantime, Red Stockings supporters, arrogant due to the phenomenal performance of their local team, began to annoy proud Chicagoans, who itched to put the smug Ohioans in their place.

In the days immediately preceding the game, Chicago fans jumped on trains for Cincinnati to cheer on the visitors. Most expected a close battle.[7] To the utter surprise and horror of Cincinnati fans, however, and to the delight of Chicagoans, the White Stockings ripped Cincinnati, 10–6. The White Stockings opened up a 6–1 lead, and the game was not even as close as the final score indicated. White Stockings fans who made the trek celebrated. So, too, did fans back home.[8]

Some of the fans who returned to Chicago on the train with the team were more than happy to stick it to the arrogant Red Stockings fans. They picked up a "month old pig, alive and grunting," outfitted it with tiny red stockings and planned to fatten it up and mockingly present it to the devastated folks of Porkopolis to ease their pain.[9] When the train returned to Chicago's old Union Depot, the White Stockings were greeted by thousands of fans who came to celebrate with the victors.[10] Chicagoans throughout the city gushed with civic pride.

The success of the team in its inaugural 1870 season encouraged the building of a new lakefront ballpark in 1871. It was built in an area of the city known as "Lake Park," located just east of Michigan Avenue between Randolph and Madison Streets. That site had once been a city dump. Today, it is part of beautiful Millennium Park.[11] The pride inspired in Chicago by baseball success would be cruelly abbreviated, however, due to the Great Fire later that year.

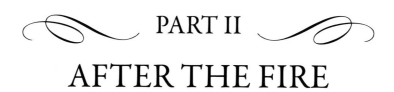

PART II
AFTER THE FIRE

Chapter 1

FROM RUIN, THE CITY REBUILDS

*If there wasn't no fire, I might have been a rich man's son
and went to Harvard and Yale—and never amounted to nothing.*
—First Ward alderman John "Bathhouse" Coughlin

On the evening of October 8, 1871, the O'Leary barn on DeKoven
Street caught fire. As the story goes, Mrs. O'Leary's cow kicked over
a lantern and started the fire. With nearly all structures in Chicago made
of wood and the city experiencing a prolonged dry spell, the city was a
tinderbox. A modest blaze could, and did, rapidly morph into an inferno.
The fire quickly spread from DeKoven Street. Before it was over, the blaze
destroyed a four-square-mile area comprising the central business district
and a substantial portion of the North Side. People were forced to flee the
fire and run for their lives. Thousands of homes were lost, hundreds of
people were dead and approximately one hundred thousand people were left
homeless.[12] Potter Palmer's new hotel burned to the ground, as did Marshall
Field's store and the *Chicago Tribune* building.[13] The fire also destroyed the
White Stockings' new lakefront ballpark.[14] So devastating and impactful was
the fire that the second star on the city's flag commemorates the event.

Some areas of the city, however, were spared, such as districts housing
manufacturing and industrial plants, as well as the South Side stockyards.[15]
The O'Leary home also survived, as did the limestone Water Tower. News
of the fire spread worldwide, generating sympathy and assistance from the
outside world. Maybe more importantly, the fire created a cause around
which Chicagoans could rally.[16]

Lithograph of burning of Tremont Hotel in Chicago Fire. *Chicago History Museum.*

O'Leary dwelling after Chicago Fire. *Chicago History Museum.*

Chicagoans did indeed rally, and a civic rebirth followed. A few days after the blaze, in its first post-fire edition, the *Chicago Tribune* played cheerleader: "Cheer Up…Chicago Shall Rise Again."[17]

And rise it did. Within the first week after the fire, thousands of temporary structures had been erected. Potter Palmer built a new Palmer House Hotel. Marshall Field constructed a new department store, and new industries, such as the retail mail-order business pioneered by Montgomery Ward and, later, another known as Sears Roebuck, started up.

By the 1880s, the city was growing and flourishing. Its population had soared to over five hundred thousand. By this time, Chicago's ideal location was not the only factor driving its astonishing population growth. St. Louis, for example, also had an ideal location and, in the early to mid-nineteenth century, was clearly the commercial center of the Midwest. The civic and business leaders of St. Louis, however, unrealistically believed that, by virtue of its advantageous location, their city was automatically predestined for future greatness. Because of that, they felt that "no special efforts were necessary."[18]

Chicago's civic leaders, on the other hand, were energetic, imaginative and more innovative than their St. Louis counterparts.[19] Willing to take risks, they aggressively capitalized on Chicago's location and made things happen, sparking the city's growth spurt. For example, not only was the retail mail-order industry a product of Chicago-born innovation, so too was the construction of the world's first steel "skyscraper," the nine-story Home Insurance Building at La Salle and Adams, in 1884.[20]

When visiting the city in 1880, a young Theodore Roosevelt was amazed by the advances he observed. He called Chicago a "marvelous City" marked by "go-aheadism," a place where one felt a "sense of big things to be done."[21] By then, Chicago had passed St. Louis in their rivalry to be the commercial center of the Midwest. Civic pride in Chicago swelled, and the city marched forward with a collective swagger.

####

While Chicago was growing by leaps and bounds, it was a dirty, violent and crime-ridden city with a well-earned and long-running reputation for lawlessness. The surging economy of the 1880s brought even more violence and crime.

On May 4, 1886, a group of anarchists, socialists and labor activists gathered in Haymarket Square—today on Randolph Street just west of Halsted—to protest working conditions and advocate for an eight-hour workday. The rally started out peacefully and remained that way until a light rain began to fall later in the evening, by which time most of the protesters had left. But when police moved in to disperse the remaining protesters, someone—still unknown today—hurled a bomb into the crowd at police. The police responded by opening fire and shooting protesters and other police officers as well. The "Haymarket Riot" left at least seven police officers dead and sixty-seven people injured, sparking outrage throughout the city.[22]

With public sentiment hostile to the anarchists, ten labor leaders who had merely organized the rally were arrested and put on trial for murder, despite no evidence connecting them to the deaths. Eight of the ten were convicted. Of those eight, seven were sentenced to death, and four of the seven sentenced to death were hanged. Seven years later, the governor acknowledged this injustice by pardoning the three surviving death row defendants, incurring the wrath of the enraged citizenry in return.[23] The Haymarket Riot and the injustice that followed exhibited to the rest of the world Chicago's proclivity toward violence and lawlessness.

////

Chicago's reputation, however, got a boost from the 1893 World's Fair, known as the Columbian Exposition, marking the 400th anniversary of Christopher Columbus's discovery of the New World. Chicago had bested New York and other cities in a competition before Congress to determine which city would host the fair. With the city's energy, imagination and appetite for innovation behind the event, it would not disappoint.

The fair opened in May 1893 on a six-hundred-acre site located on the South Side near Jackson Park. The site included, among other attractions, a newly constructed building that today houses the Museum of Science and Industry. Chicago innovation was on display with the world's first Ferris wheel, as well as Chicago architect Daniel Burnham's magnificent "White City."

The White City consisted of neoclassical buildings with glimmering, electrified white stucco siding. Electric lights amazingly lit up the streets, allowing fair visitors an extraordinary, first-time peek at the future. When

Daniel Burnham. *Chicago History Museum.*

lit up at night, the white buildings were stunning, providing an almost magical aura. Burnham's White City gave Chicagoans a semblance of culture, art and beauty that had previously been woefully lacking.

Born in Henderson, New York, in 1846, Daniel H. Burnham had moved to Chicago with his family in 1855. Initially, he took an entry position in the architecture field. That didn't last long, and he moved to Nevada, where he tried his luck at mining. That didn't work out. He also tried a run for the U.S. Senate, but that, too, didn't work out. By 1870 he had returned to Chicago.[24]

In 1872, shortly after the Great Chicago Fire, Burnham went back into architecture. With all the reconstruction going on in the city, it was a good and timely move, and he was able to find his true calling. Earning a reputation for honesty and the ability to find solutions for his business clients' problems, Burnham worked on major buildings and projects throughout the city. He also became one of the chief proponents of the emerging City Beautiful movement, which sought to fuse the functionality of architecture work with art and beauty, exemplified by the White City. The World's Fair enhanced Burnham's reputation, not only locally but also internationally, as a great city planner and architect.

Overall, the 1893 World's Fair was a phenomenal success, with more than 27 million visitors attending over 179 days.[25] So successful was the fair that the third star on the flag of the City of Chicago commemorates the event.

Chapter 2

BASEBALL AROUND THE TURN OF THE TWENTIETH CENTURY

You're a liar. There ain't no "Hotel Episode" in Detroit!
—eccentric turn-of-the-twentieth-century pitcher Rube Waddell, on hearing that
he was being fined $100 for his part in a hotel episode in Detroit

Major League Baseball has changed with the times in numerous ways. For example, at the dawn of the twentieth century, Black ballplayers were not welcome in the majors. This was traceable to 1884, when Chicago White Stockings manager Cap Anson allegedly yelled about a Black ballplayer, "Get that n***** off the field!"[26] A man of considerable influence, Anson's refusal is said to have resulted in a "gentlemen's agreement" among baseball owners to exclude Blacks from baseball for decades—until Jackie Robinson took the field for Brooklyn in 1947.

In the early 1900s, with commercial air travel not yet available, teams traveled from city to city via train and often utilized sleeper cars. With travel limited to the rails, there were no major league teams west of St. Louis. It would be fifty years before the Dodgers and Giants moved from Brooklyn and New York, respectively, to California. With the western part of the country practically off-limits in the early 1900s, there were only sixteen major league teams—eight in the National League and eight in the newly formed American League.

Back then, electric lighting was still a recent development, and stadiums were not equipped with lights. Games were played during the day, usually starting at 3:00 p.m. in Chicago. Of course, a fan could not track his team's progress on the Internet or watch on TV. Neither had been invented; even commercial radio would not be available until 1920. Instead, if one wanted to follow his or her team in the first decade of the twentieth century, the only ways were to read about the game in the local newspaper or see it in person. On the positive side, without lengthy between-innings "media" breaks for commercials, games were often played in two hours or less.

Like the times themselves, baseball back then was often rowdy and brawling. It was not uncommon for base runners to slide into second base with spikes high, intending to cut the fielder. Bench-clearing brawls or malicious jeering along the benches were also standard. Hazing, especially of rookies by established veterans, usually was not friendly and at times could be plain cruel.

Political correctness would have been a foreign concept to players and fans back then. The language used by players and coaches was often crude and offensive and could easily be overheard by the fans. And the spectators were no saints, either. At times, they would throw glass bottles at opposing players and even the umpires.

In 1900, only one umpire worked a game, although that increased to two in a few years. Base runners would, to borrow the phrase of Detroit Tigers star outfielder Sam Crawford, "run with one eye on the ball and one eye on the umpire." In other words, if a runner was approaching third and the umpire's attention was focused on first, the runner would shortcut the basepath and not bother to touch third at all.[27] That wasn't always foolproof, however. Once, as the story goes, umpire Tim Hurst had his attention diverted from home plate, and a runner came in to score without a play being made on him. Nonetheless, the umpire called the runner out. "You got here too quick," Hurst said.[28]

Back then, pitchers were expected to throw complete games, and modern-day "pitch counts" were unheard of, as were thirteen-man pitching staffs. If an overworked pitcher developed a sore arm, management's loss of its minimal investment in him was not a source of great concern. Nonetheless, pitchers enjoyed some huge advantages over hitters that they do not have today. Most obvious was the composition of the ball, with a rubber center, not the rubber-and-cork center used later. This "dead" ball was much less lively and was not conducive to home runs. The period from 1900 to 1919 became known as the "Deadball Era."

Pitchers were able to enhance their advantage in the Deadball Era by throwing "spitballs," which were allowed at the time. The pitcher might spit on the ball or use a lubricant such as Vaseline, which he might keep in the bill of his cap. Wetting or greasing the ball affected its weight on one side and caused it to move in an unpredictable manner, making it harder to hit.

With pitchers holding the advantage, home runs were few and far between. Offenses instead relied on what became known as the "Inside Game," which featured bunts, squeezes, stolen bases, proper baserunning and sliding and use of the hit-and-run.

Player safety was not a major priority. Batters did not wear helmets, leaving them exposed to severe concussions or even death if struck in the head by a fastball. Catchers were also left vulnerable. While they wore protective masks, catchers did not begin to use shin guards with regularity until 1908. Fielders were at high risk as well. In even earlier times, the prevailing attitude had been that wearing a mitt made you a wimp and that mangled fingers and broken bones demonstrated a fielder's toughness. That attitude began to change, resulting in fielders using small mitts barely larger than their hands.

Player pay is another big difference between baseball today and the sport a century ago. Most ballplayers back then were paid modest, if not meager, wages. In 1908, the average major league salary was $2,500, compared with the millions that the average player receives today.[29] Players back then were at an extreme economic disadvantage, because free agency as we know it today did not exist. Rather, the infamous "reserve clause" in the standard players' contracts effectively allowed management to renew its rights to a player's services year after year for as long as management wanted, even for the life of a player's career. Players were left with little bargaining power to earn a market-based salary, making it necessary for many players to take second jobs in the offseason to make ends meet. That, in turn, did not allow players the opportunity for the off-season conditioning so routine for today's ballplayers.

Finally, the Cubs in the early twentieth century were not North-Siders; they were West-Siders. They played their home games at West Side Grounds at Taylor and Wolcott (then Lincoln Street) and would not move to what is now known as Wrigley Field until 1916.

Chapter 3

CHICAGO AROUND THE TURN OF THE TWENTIETH CENTURY

I have struck a city—a real city—and they call it Chicago....I urgently desire
never to see it again. It is inhabited by savages.
—Rudyard Kipling, 1891

By the turn of the twentieth century, Chicago's population had grown to 1.6 million. It was now the second-largest city in America, passing Philadelphia and trailing only New York.

Two days into the new century, the city once again displayed its penchant for innovation. Prior to 1900, polluted water from the Chicago River flowing into Lake Michigan contaminated the city's water supply. The city, however, had a solution: reverse the flow of the Chicago River to cause unclean river water to flow away from Lake Michigan, keeping the lake water potable. On January 2, 1900, the city completed the creation of the twenty-eight-mile Sanitary & Ship Canal, a prodigious engineering accomplishment. The contaminated river water then flowed away from the lake, into the canal, west toward the Des Plaines River, then to the Illinois River and ultimately to the Mississippi River.

Of course, before the canal was completed, the possibility of all of Chicago's sewage flowing to St. Louis drew the ire of the citizens of the Gateway City, and Chicago city leaders feared that St. Louis would seek an injunction. However, the canal was opened secretly, allowing Chicago to preserve its clean water supply.

View north on State Street at Madison in early 1900s. *Chicago History Museum.*

//////

"Paradoxical" might aptly describe Chicago at the beginning of the twentieth century. Despite its incredible growth and impressive achievements, it was still a dirty, dangerous and depressing place, and life for most of its residents was hard. For most Chicago workers, their jobs required sixty hours or more per week of difficult and dangerous labor for meager pay, and in many families, the children had to work to make ends meet. In his 1904 work *The Shame of the Cities*, reporter Lincoln Steffens said that Chicago was "first in violence, deepest in dirt, lawlessness, unlovely, ill-smelling, irreverent, new—an overgrown gawk of a village, the 'tough' among cities, a spectacle for the nation."[30] Squalor, corruption and violence pervaded daily life. Thick factory smoke filled the air and darkened the skies. Dirt, dinginess and ramshackle, dilapidated structures were everywhere,[31] and a coating of grease covered the surface of the Chicago River.[32] Powerful, disgusting odors were emitted from piles of garbage and, near the stockyards, from decaying animal carcasses.[33]

Certainly the Wild West had nothing on Chicago. In 1905, there were eight thousand saloons in Chicago, approximately one saloon for every two hundred adults and children.[34] These establishments were definitely not family places, and some posed hidden dangers to their customers. One infamous saloon, Mickey Finn's, sold a spiked cocktail that would knock its drinker unconscious. By the time the victim came to, he had been robbed, stripped of most of his clothing and left alone in an alley.

Corruption was rampant, especially in the Chicago City Council. In his 1894 book *If Christ Came to Chicago*, visiting minister Reverend William T. Stead painted a vivid portrait of the aldermen of the city council, describing them as "swindlers and scoundrels sitting in the center of the whole machine and treating their duties and their trust as means by which they can fill their own pockets."[35] Sugarcoating nothing, Stead called them the "swine of our civilization."[36] So pervasive was corruption in the city council that Stead claimed he could find only ten honest aldermen among its sixty-eight members.[37]

What primarily fueled Chicago City Council corruption were "protection payments" from vice establishments, including those engaging in prostitution and gambling. During the days of the 1893 World's Fair, a vice district sprang up not far from the fair's location, occupied by brothels, gambling houses, seedy saloons, drug dens and other places of decadence. Known as the "Levee District," it was located in the southern part of the First Ward just north of Twenty-Second Street along the east bank of the Chicago River. There, cops looked the other way, and vice laws were rarely enforced.

There were more than one thousand brothels in the Levee District, ranging from the ornate to the sparse. The most notorious brothel was the Everleigh Club. Opened in 1900, it was run by Minna and her sister Ada Everleigh out of a massive brownstone mansion at 2131 South Dearborn. While most brothels were looked down on, the Everleigh Club was considered with high regard. It became the most famous brothel in Chicago and the biggest brothel in the world, featuring the world's highest-paid prostitutes.[38] The Everleigh Club had fifty bedrooms and six ornate parlors and was richly decorated with tapestries, Oriental rugs and impressionist paintings. One room featured a waterfall. The "Gold Room" upstairs contained fishbowls, spittoons and a piano, all rimmed or made with gold. Customers were entertained by performing orchestras and were served by chefs, porters and other waitstaff. Dinner prices started at $50 a person at a time when sirloin steak cost the average consumer $0.14 per pound.[39] The $50 dinner price was without female companionship, which could cost as much as an extra $500.[40] Expectations were that every visitor would spend at least $50 a night; and those who did not were not welcome back.[41]

In stark contrast to the opulence and amenities of the Everleigh Club, some of the brothels in the Levee District were infamous "panel houses." In the bedrooms of these houses, a chair was placed against a wall for the customer to hang his jacket on. That wall, however, contained a secret sliding panel. While the customer was otherwise distracted, the establishment's owner accessed the panel from behind the wall, and the valuables in the customer's jacket pockets disappeared without the customer knowing until after he had left the establishment.[42]

Violent crimes such as murder, burglary and theft were widespread. Just walking down the street posed a danger. Men openly carried pistols and knives in public, and fistfighting and brawling commonly occurred on the streets. Boys, in fact, were *expected* to fight. A so-called leading authority of the time said that, for their own growth, health and well-being, young boys should get into at least one fight per day!

Fistfighting and brawling youngsters back then could identify with a famous and powerful role model who had earlier earned a reputation as a brawler. Theodore Roosevelt, the president of the United States, had, for most of his life, embraced a good fight. He had been a boxer in college and took up various martial arts, some of which he continued to practice while president. As a younger man, Roosevelt was known to have floored a person who verbally ridiculed him, and he was a central figure in a western barroom brawl during which the future president knocked cold his adversary.[43]

The president's penchant for pugilism nicely fit in with rowdy and brawling Chicago. In April 1903, Roosevelt visited the city and gave a speech at the Auditorium Theater.[44] There, he made this famous statement: "There is an old adage which runs: 'speak softly and carry a big stick; you will go far.'"[45] The "old adage" neatly suited the city and time.

//////

While organized crime figures owned many of the Levee District's vice establishments, the true "bosses" of the district were First Ward aldermen John "Bathhouse" Coughlin and five-foot, two-inch saloonkeeper Michael "Hinky Dink" Kenna.[46]

Left: Alderman Michael Kenna. *Chicago History Museum.*

Below: Alderman John Coughlin. *Chicago History Museum.*

Coughlin was born of Irish immigrant parents and raised in a poor Irish section of the city in what is today's West Loop. His father owned a grocery store that was destroyed by the Great Chicago Fire, so young John had to work to help support the family. As an eleven-year-old, he took a job as a "rubber," giving massages in a Turkish bathhouse, from which his nickname was derived. He worked hard and saved his money. Eventually, he bought a bathhouse of his own, then several more, as well as a saloon.[47]

Coughlin was likable and outgoing—the life of the party. With his modest upbringing, he could easily relate to the common man. Coughlin's business experience, together with his outgoing and "man of the people" persona, allowed him to make many useful political contacts and friends. In 1892, Bathhouse leveraged these assets to win election as alderman of Chicago's First Ward.

Like Coughlin, Kenna learned what it took to make money on his own at an early age, selling newspapers at age ten and buying his own newsstand at twelve. In adulthood, he owned a saloon on Clark Street called the Workingmen's Exchange. It was known for its nearly one-hundred-foot-long bar—supposedly the world's largest—and the huge schooners of beer served there.[48] While the saloon occupied the first floor of the Clark Street building, Kenna ran a gambling parlor upstairs.

Kenna had a soft spot for those who were down on their luck, and his saloon was a haven for tramps, the homeless and criminals. In one week during the cheerless depression winter of 1893–94, he provided free lunches for eight thousand such men.[49] Kenna helped them find jobs and got them out of police trouble. He came to realize, however, that his generosity could be the source of personal benefit, both politically and monetarily.[50]

In 1894, under pressure from reformers, the city started to hassle gamblers, and this cut into Hinky Dink's gambling profits. To protect his interests before the Chicago City Council, he convinced Alderman Coughlin that, with Kenna's help, Coughlin could win reelection in 1894 as First Ward alderman and that they should work together toward that end.[51] The cunning Kenna had come up with a nefarious plan for a Coughlin victory and was ready to get to work on it.

////

"There have been elections in Chicago and there have been elections, but yesterday's…was a world-beater," proclaimed the *Tribune* after the 1894 First

Ward aldermanic election.[52] It was a campaign fought with weapons, fists and bribes as much as with votes. Opposing the incumbent Coughlin in the 1894 election were two opponents: Republican Irving Pearce, who had not previously held public office; and Democrat Michael "The Clock" Skakel, a gambling-house proprietor.

Kenna's election plan included taking advantage of his providing favors and benevolence to the downtrodden by recruiting them and taking them to a voting place with ballots pre-marked for Coughlin. The patrons would receive from fifty cents to one dollar if they brought back new ballots, so that the whole scheme could be repeated. Just prior to the election, according to plan, vagrants and homeless people surged into the First Ward. Kenna, along with his cronies, housed them in any possible place—saloons, brothels, empty buildings. At his saloon, he supplied them with beer served in large schooners. In turn, he got them registered to vote in the First Ward. In fact, more people were registered in this normally low-profile aldermanic election than were registered for the relatively high-profile mayoral election the previous December.[53]

In the meantime, Mayor John Hopkins was concerned that Coughlin and Skakel might split the Democratic vote and thus hand the election to the Republican, Irving Pearce. When Hopkins asked Skakel to withdraw, Skakel in effect told Hopkins to take a hike. Hopkins then told Skakel that he, the mayor, could not be responsible for what might follow.[54]

After that, Coughlin received the full and brutal support of the police in the First Ward. Coughlin's goons would be free to violently attack anyone wearing a Skakel badge, without intervention from the police.

When the voting booths opened on Election Day, Hinky Dink Kenna's band of vagabond voters went into action, according to Kenna's plan. To provide protection for Kenna's voters, and for added muscle, Kenna procured for Coughlin a group of street thugs that included two bouncers, a bridge tender, a former prizefighter and the brother of one of the bouncers.[55] They belonged to the notorious Quincy Boys street gang.

By 6:00 a.m. on Election Day, April 4, 1894, Coughlin's thugs were armed with billy clubs, blackjacks, brass knuckles and pistols.[56] They traversed the First Ward in a carriage, determined to find and beat up any Skakel supporter they could find. Throughout the ward and throughout the day, Skakel supporters took bloody beatings from Coughlin's thugs. To make matters worse, the police hauled the battered Skakel supporters to jail.

At the Sixth Precinct voting place, the Quincy Boys spotted a Skakel supporter named John Duffy, whom they beat to a pulp. While being beaten,

Duffy turned to a nearby policeman for help. The cop told Duffy that the beating he was enduring served him right for supporting Skakel. The officer refused to intervene.[57]

At the next polling place, the Quincy Boys' wagon came upon a Skakel supporter named "Jumbo." According to the *Tribune*, Coughlin's thugs went after Jumbo "like a hungry hyena in a traveling circus making an evening meal of raw steak." Jumbo was hit hard about the head with revolvers and billy clubs. He appeared to fear for his life, and he tried to escape by running, screaming for help. Unfortunately, he ran straight into a policeman. The officer whacked Jumbo over the head with a billy club. Then, bloodied and beaten, Jumbo was tossed into a police wagon and locked up at the Harrison Street Station.[58]

At Kenna's saloon, which also served as a polling place, an African American male was seen wearing a Skakel button. He was beaten silly with blackjacks and arrested.[59]

In front of the McCoy Hotel, a Coughlin goon, spotting an apparent Skakel supporter, pulled out a revolver and fired a shot, which hit the front of the hotel, where hotel patrons and other citizens were convened, causing great consternation among everyone in the vicinity. A police officer who witnessed the shooting approached the gun-shooting Coughlin goon but made no effort to arrest him. Instead, the officer suggested that he disappear by taking a walk around the block.[60]

Another account involving the McCoy Hotel described a carriage full of Coughlin thugs spotting a group of Skakel supporters. According to this account, shots were fired from the carriage at the Skakelites. The Coughlin gang then jumped from their carriage and charged at the Skakel supporters, who retreated into the lobby. There, a full-fledged brawl ensued. Guns were fired, and clubs were swung. Furniture was upended, and the hotel's walls and woodwork were shot up. Before the dust cleared, the Skakel supporters lie bloodied and beaten on the lobby floor, with the Coughlin supporters kicking them while they were down. When the police arrived, they were able to distinguish members of each group by the badges they were wearing. The police arrested the battered and beaten Skakel supporters and hauled them to the Harrison Street Police Station.[61] The Coughlin supporters, who initiated the mayhem, were left to go about their business.

The violence continued later that day when a near riot ensued off State Street as supporters from both camps ran into one another. A significant crowd gathered to eye the confrontation. Billy clubs and blackjacks swung, revolvers were fired, razors were used and terrified onlookers scattered, stalling cable cars and causing chaos in the streets. Riot police were called, and police began clubbing indiscriminately both belligerents and innocent bystanders. Supporters of both Coughlin and Skakel were injured. In the end, while the injured Skakel supporters were arrested and sent to the police station, the injured Coughlin belligerents were taken to the hospital.[62]

After the votes were counted, Coughlin, the beneficiary of Hinky Dink's crooked and violent election tactics and the sordid support from Chicago's finest, emerged as the winner.

////

After the 1894 election, Kenna and Coughlin continued to work together. Starting in 1897, when each Chicago ward began having two aldermen, Kenna would be elected and join Coughlin as the First Ward's two aldermen. Because their personalities were so different, Coughlin and Kenna formed a political odd couple. Kenna was quiet and reserved but shrewd, street-smart and politically astute. He generally kept a low profile. He would become the behind-the-scenes brains of the operation.

On the other hand, with his likability, outgoing personality and many contacts, Coughlin became the front man. He had nowhere near the smarts of Hinky Dink and often exhibited outlandish behavior. For one thing, he often wore outrageous and colorful clothing (for example, in pink and yellow, and those were just his gloves and shoes to go with green pants).[63] Coughlin also fancied himself an aspiring poet, but his work was terrible. One of his poems is titled "She Sleeps by the Drainage Canal"; another is "Why Build the Lovely Lake So Close to the Horrible Shore." A third poem, "Ode to a Bathtub," went like this:

> *Some go to ballgames for pleasure, others go bobbing for eels,*
> *Some find delight in making money, especially in real estate deals,*
> *I care not for ball games or fishing, or money unless to buy grub*
> *But I'd walk forty miles before breakfast to roll in the porcelain tub.*[64]

After reading his poetry, some people thought Coughlin was dim-witted, or worse. In fact, Mayor Carter Harrison II once asked Kenna if Coughlin was crazy or on drugs. Kenna could only reply, "To tell the God's truth, Mayor, they ain't found a name for it yet."[65]

Coughlin constructed an elaborate zoo and amusement park on property he owned in Colorado Springs. One of the animals in Coughlin's Colorado Springs zoo was an elephant he had purchased from Chicago's Lincoln Park Zoo. The elephant, Princess Alice, was very popular with the zoo visitors.

One winter, Princess Alice caught a cold that lingered for some time. Coughlin recommended that she be given what he took to cure a cold: whiskey. With that recommendation, the zookeepers didn't cheat Princess Alice. They gave her a whole quart of whiskey, and it worked like a charm, curing her cold. But it left her with an unquenchable craving for the drink. When the quantities of whiskey given to Princess Alice by her zookeepers were no longer enough for her, she began looking for visitors with flasks. She would beg for drinks from them, and when whiskey was given to her, she would take it, find a comfortable spot to lie down and fall asleep.[66]

Together, Coughlin and Kenna did not hesitate to take what they could, legally or not. For example, at one point, aldermen were given allowances from public funds to hire and pay for personal secretaries, whether or not secretarial services were truly needed. Apparently not completely satisfied with this benefit, Coughlin promptly hired Kenna as his secretary, and Kenna hired Coughlin. Both kept the secretarial salary in addition to their aldermanic pay.[67]

From the Levee District's saloons, gambling halls and brothels—including the Everleigh Club—"protection money" poured into the coffers of Kenna and Coughlin. They typically received $25 from the small houses and up to $100 for larger ones—more if the houses sold drinks or allowed gambling. The aldermen also charged substantial fees for clearing citizens' indictments.

Paradoxically, while both men could be kindhearted, throughout their decades of overseeing the city's First Ward they took enormous amounts of graft and protection money out of the district. They eventually became possibly the most powerful duo in city history.

Chapter 4

FROM "WHITE STOCKINGS" TO "COLTS" TO "CUBS"

Do it my way or meet me after the game.
—Cubs player-manager Frank Chance

Two years after the Great Chicago Fire, the White Stockings resumed play, and in 1876, they joined the newly created baseball league that later became known as the National League. The White Stockings won the new league's first pennant. A few years later, from 1880 to 1891, they enjoyed one of the most successful periods in the franchise's history. The team, managed by future Hall of Famer Cap Anson, won five of the first eleven pennants and had eleven top-three finishes in that period. It would be the franchise's first dynasty, but not the last.

By 1887, however, as the team fell on tougher times and consisted of younger players, the newspapers began referring to the club as "Anson's Colts." In the next few years, "Colts" stuck as their official name; "White Stockings" was out. The change of name, however, did not help the team's performance on the field. The nineteenth century closed with fourteen straight years of the Colts failing to win another NL pennant. Tommy Burns replaced Cap Anson as manager in 1898 and had two winning seasons. In neither season did the Colts come close to a title.

As the twentieth century dawned, times became even more challenging for the Colts. In 1900, a new and rival league was formed, the American League. Player raids by the new league followed. The raids depleted the roster of the Colts to such an extent that sportswriters jokingly referred to

Left: Cubs manager Frank Selee. *Chicago History Museum*.

Right: Cubs outfielder Jimmy Slagle. *Chicago History Museum*.

them as the "Remnants." By 1901, the Colts had nearly hit rock bottom, finishing with a dismal .381 winning percentage and one of the worst records in franchise history.

After the 1901 season, the Colts needed to rebuild, so owner Jim Hart hired Boston Beaneaters manager Frank Selee, who had already won five pennants for the Beaneaters and was well respected throughout baseball, to oversee the rebuild. In fact, Selee "was one of the first master evaluators of talent in baseball history."[68] Selee took over as manager in 1902. As we shall see, Hart could not have picked a better person for the job.

Coming over from Boston prior to the 1902 season along with Selee was outfielder Jimmy Slagle, who became the center fielder and lead-off man. Slagle was a good defensive player, possessing a great arm. He was known by more than one nickname—in fact, several. He was known as "Rabbit" because of his speed. He was so fast that, in his tiny hometown of Worthville, Pennsylvania, the townsfolk told stories of Jimmy, on returning home to visit, standing in front of his house, throwing a ball over the roof and running around back in time to catch it on the fly.[69] Also known as the "Human Mosquito" for his "peskiness"[70] and "Shorty" for obvious reasons, Slagle once said: "I was only 5'6 and batted left-handed and when I crouched over the plate there wasn't much for a pitcher to throw at. In fact, I used to walk so often that one of our pitchers once said that I was the only player he ever saw who stole first base."[71]

////

One of the Colts players Selee inherited was starting catcher Johnny Kling. As a teen, Kling worked in a Kansas City pool hall and became quite proficient at billiards, a skill that would serve him well later in life. He then bounced around semipro baseball and the minors, including as a catcher in Rockford, before coming to the Colts in 1900.

Kling was highly intelligent. He learned all the tendencies and weaknesses of opposing hitters and relished the challenge of outsmarting them. He handled pitchers brilliantly, would often throw from the crouch position and had a rocket of an arm.[72] It was no coincidence that, when the Cub pitching staff led the NL for three straight years (1905–7), Kling was calling the signals behind the plate.[73] He was also tough as nails. Once, the Giants' Win Mercer collided forcefully with Kling at the plate in an attempt to knock Kling over, but it was Mercer who was knocked out cold and carried away.[74]

Kling's teammates later recognized his enormous value. In 1910, future Hall of Fame teammate Johnny Evers referred to him as "the greatest catcher the game ever has known,"[75] and Hall of Fame pitcher Mordecai Brown said that he never saw Kling "call a wrong pitch."[76] Pitcher Ed Reulbach praised him as "one of the greatest catchers who ever wore a mask."[77]

When Selee took over as manager, he also inherited the backup catcher, a promising, college-bred son of a banker from Fresno, California, named Frank Chance. His father's dream had been that Frank would follow in his footsteps as a banker, but his father died when Frank was only fourteen. During Frank's California college days, he played baseball as a catcher. Chicago scouts Cal McVey and Bill Lange had both seen Chance play and were impressed. It wasn't long before Chicago manager Cap Anson received from Lange the following scouting report on Chance: "Here's the most promising player I ever saw. Someday he'll be a wonder."[78]

When Frank ultimately decided to pursue a baseball career and sign with Chicago, his family, especially his mother, did not take it well. That was not unusual in those days. Baseball players were generally seen by the public as crude, rough-and-tumble scalawags, and most parents of aspiring ballplayers preferred that their sons choose another calling.

Opposite: Cubs catcher Johnny Kling. *Chicago History Museum.*

Left: Cubs player-manager Frank Chance. *Chicago History Museum.*

Notwithstanding his family's objections, Chance joined the Colts in 1898 as a backup catcher and made a good first impression. One writer said of Chance, "When he was given the opportunity to work behind the bat, he stopped the pitched balls with the tips of his fingers, the foul tips with his knees, and the wild pitches with the top of his head." According to the writer, Chance "could take punishment and come back for more."[79] In fact, despite his white-collar upbringing, Chance would grow to be a tough and fearless brawler who once got into a fight with heavyweight champion James J. Corbett. As a manager, Chance was known to tell his players, "Do it my way or meet me after the game."

Having inherited two talented catchers, Kling and Chance, Selee had a dilemma: how to best utilize, and get the most out of, both. Recognizing that Chance was a solid hitter and an adept base stealer, Selee decided to convert Chance to first base in 1902.[80] Originally, Chance resisted, not wanting to make the move, but Selee eventually persuaded him to do so. As a first baseman, Chance would go on to a Hall of Fame career.

Having resolved his dilemma with Kling and Chance, Selee then went to work on rebuilding the ball club. That basically involved a two-step process. Selee orchestrated the first step: bringing in talented young players and developing them over time—a youth movement. Second, when those young players had developed sufficiently to contend for a title, Selee's successor went out and obtained quality veteran players to plug up any remaining holes. It was a process not unlike one Theo Epstein used to build the Cubs' 2016 World Series team more than a century later.[81]

The Cubs Rebuild, Step 1: Selee's Youth Movement (1902–5)

In 1902, Selee's youth movement caused the *Chicago Daily News* to refer to the ballclub as the Cubs. The name stuck. This stage began with the acquisition of two future Hall-of-Fame infielders, Joe Tinker and Johnny Evers.

Joe Tinker grew up dirt-poor in a "shabby little house" in Kansas City.[82] As a boy, he played baseball in vacant lots, and his talent was so apparent that he started playing professional ball at the age of ten for thirty-five dollars a month. By the time he was twenty-one, Tinker had played in numerous minor league venues, including in Kansas City (where he was a teammate of Johnny Kling before the two were later reunited with the Cubs), Denver and Portland, Oregon.

Playing for Portland, his salary was seventy-five dollars a month. When his 1901 season there was over, Tinker paid for his train fare back to Kansas City and realized that he had only seventy-five dollars left to spend over the entire winter. He saved money that winter by staying at his parents' home, but they were in no position to help him financially. They barely had enough to get by themselves. So young Joe was forced to get by over the winter on that same seventy-five dollars. That would prove to be a daunting challenge, especially if, at the same time, he also hoped to date a young lady.

Soon after he arrived back in Kansas City, Tinker met and began to court a "little blue-eyed girl." Today, the average young man facing a cash shortage and wanting to treat his girl to a nice evening on the town just pulls out his (or his parents') credit card, and the cash problem is solved—at least in the short term. But in those days, easy credit was not available to the extent it is today, so Joe Tinker had little choice but to put himself on an austere budget for the entirety of that offseason. Of the seventy-five dollars he had saved, he allowed himself five dollars a week to spend, and of that, he would spend one dollar a week to entertain his girl. Monday night was "date night" for the couple. "Every Monday night the two young folks attended a vaudeville theater. $.50 went for the pair of tickets, $.25 for a box of candy, $.20 for carfare, and the odd nickel was spent for a package of gum."[83]

While he was not able to impress his girl with expensive gifts or promises of an extravagant lifestyle, Tinker was usually cheerful, laughed often and had a great sense of humor.[84] In short, he was a good guy who was fun to be around.

For the Tinker family, luxuries were certainly not in the budget, and by Christmas morning, the usually upbeat Joe found himself lying on his bed

Cubs Joe Tinker and John Evers. *Chicago History Museum.*

in his parents' little house, lamenting that he and his parents could not even afford the small luxury of a turkey for Christmas dinner. While Joe lay there, his mother walked into his room and handed him an envelope from James A. Hart, owner of the Chicago National League ball club. Tinker ripped open the envelope and found a check for $300, along with a letter saying that Chicago wanted him to play for them in the 1902 season at a salary of $1,800. The check was an advance payment. Jubilant, Tinker ran out and bought a turkey dinner for him and his parents.

Before leaving Kansas City to join the Chicago team, Joe told his girl that he hoped he would be able to propose marriage someday but that he did not want to do so until he could afford to give her the same lifestyle she enjoyed at her parents' home. According to *Tribune* writer James Crusinberry, "He asked her how much he thought a young man should have before he gets married, and her answer was: 'My mother says a man ought to have $2,000 before he gets married.'"[85] That sounded like a huge amount to Tinker, but being resourceful and thrifty, he was determined to get it, no matter how long it took.

In 1902, Tinker came up to Chicago as a third baseman, but Selee recognized that his defensive abilities were more conducive to playing shortstop. As was the case with Chance, Tinker adamantly objected to a change in position and at first refused to make any move. But, as he had done with Chance, Selee ultimately prevailed, and twenty-two-year-old Joe Tinker became a regular at short for the Cubs.

Tinker found it rough going at first, as he led the league in errors his first season. But he continued to show improvement and received a nice raise for the 1903 season. In the meantime, he had been saving from his 1902 salary with the Cubs to afford to get married. After the 1903 season, his bank account had reached $1,950. Even though he was $50 short of the $2,000 target, the wedding took place that offseason, and his "blue-eyed girl became Mrs. Tinker."[86]

Eventually, Tinker became known as one of the slickest-fielding shortstops of his time. Among his contemporaries, he was rated second only to legendary Hall of Famer Honus Wagner as a fielder. On the other hand, Tinker was often criticized as a light hitter, and indeed his lifetime batting average is only .263. But he was a tremendous clutch hitter. He was also fast and aggressive on the bases. He would end up stealing 304 bases in his lifetime as a Cub, fourth-highest on the all-time club list. He stole a career-high 41 bases in 1904. On June 28, 1910, he stole home twice in one game, an 11–1 win over the Reds.[87]

////

Around Labor Day 1902, nineteen-year-old, 105-pound Johnny Evers arrived to play next to Tinker at second base. The Cubs paid $250 for Evers's contract, an investment that eventually proved to be one of the most rewarding in Cubs history.

The son of a saloonkeeper, Evers came from a working-class Irish family and had little more than an eighth-grade education. He was nicknamed "Trojan" because of his Troy, New York birthplace and "the Crab" because of his surly disposition, foul mouth, temper and, obviously, crabbiness. Many of the people Evers dealt with considered him a pain in the behind, and he rarely got along with others. That would even include his jovial future double-play partner with the Cubs, Joe Tinker.

Evers compensated for his short stature by hustling and doing whatever it took to win.[88] He was a "bundle of nerves" and an intense, "fiery competitor."[89] On one occasion, Evers's nerves made him so uptight that Manager Chance ordered him to go out that night and get drunk. Tinker complied, and the next day, he had two hits.[90]

While Evers's lack of formal education contrasted markedly with the college-educated Chance, Evers was just as baseball smart, if not smarter, than Chance. In fact, Evers developed a reputation as one of the smartest and most "heads-up" players of his day.

After coming up to the Cubs late in the 1902 season, Evers hit a mediocre .222 over the final few weeks of the season when filling a nonstarting role. The fact that he was small did not make life any easier for him at first, as he was ridiculed and bullied by his teammates. One time, instead of allowing Evers to ride inside the team bus, his teammates made him sit on the roof.[91] More notably, he became part of history on September 15, 1902, when the first Tinker-to-Evers-to-Chance double play was recorded.[92]

⫻⫻⫻

During the 1903–4 offseason, the Cubs added a former Indiana coal miner who had suffered a childhood injury to his pitching hand, Mordecai "Three Finger" Brown. At the age of seven, he was playing on his uncle's farm when his right hand became mangled in a corn shredder. His thumb and pinky were both permanently impaired, and his index finger was amputated above the second knuckle. Shortly after that, he fell and broke his other fingers while chasing either a rabbit or a hog, depending on which

Cubs pitcher Mordecai Brown. *Chicago History Museum.*

account one reads. This left him with "a bent middle finger, a paralyzed little finger, and a stump where the index finger used to be."[93]

As Brown grew into young adulthood in Indiana, he toiled as a coal miner by day, and on evenings and weekends he played for the company baseball team. Originally, he was a third baseman, but when forced to pitch in an emergency, Brown realized the benefits that could be had from his childhood tragedies. Brown was able to spin his pitches off his middle finger, causing the ball to sink and tail away from batters. "That old paw served me pretty well in its time. It gave me a firmer grip on the ball, so I could spin it over the hump. It gave me a greater dip," Brown later remarked.[94] When Brown was asked if pitching without an index finger was a disadvantage, he responded, "I don't know. I've never done it the other way."[95]

After two successful seasons in the minors pitching with his deformed right hand, Brown began his major league career with the St. Louis Cardinals in 1903 but won only nine games for them. Not foreseeing stardom for Brown, the Cardinals traded him to the Cubs for one of their top pitchers, Jack Taylor, who twice had won twenty games. Cub fans were incensed. But the wisdom of Selee's move soon became apparent. Brown eventually became a baseball Hall of Famer and was recognized by many as the greatest pitcher in Cubs history.

In the meantime, the infamous corn shredder that brought Brown such grief was put on display and became a popular tourist attraction in Brown's hometown of Nyesville, Indiana.

Cubs right-fielder Frank Schulte. *Chicago History Museum.*

Selee enhanced his youth movement by relying on astute scouting to identify and sign amateur players. One such addition made during the 1903–4 offseason was outfielder Frank "Wildfire" Schulte.[96]

Schulte would become one of the top sluggers in the game. But had it been up to his father, Frank never would have played baseball. His dad was a German immigrant who became a successful contractor. When Wildfire was sixteen, his dad offered him the huge sum—by those days' standards—of $1,000 if he would give up the game of baseball. Schulte turned down his dad's offer, and the Cubs signed him three years later.

Schulte was a fun-loving guy off the field. He loved Thoroughbred horse racing, and he even purchased his own racehorse, named "Wildfire." The name of Schulte's horse eventually became the genesis of Schulte's own nickname. Schulte also enjoyed drinking with legendary *Tribune* sportswriter Ring Lardner. Eventually, Lardner based many of his sports novels on Schulte's persona.[97]

By the end of the 1904 season, Selee's rebuilding efforts were starting to reap rewards. The Cubs finished in second place, their best finish in thirteen years. Not only had Selee's talent-evaluation skills allowed him to find the optimal positions for Chance and Tinker and bring in top young players like Brown and Schulte, he also instilled a positive, hustling, winning mentality,

Cubs pitcher Ed Reulbach. *Chicago History Museum.*

so important for championship teams. He felt that if the Cubs played hard on every play, much like the defending Giants had the year before, the team had a chance to contend with New York for the title in 1905. He advocated maximum hustle all the time, stating, "It's the man who runs out every hit who is always on edge and wide awake, but it appears to have luck."[98]

With more rebuilding still to be done, early in the 1905 season, the Cubs added a pitcher, rookie "Big Ed" Reulbach, who had pitched at the University of Notre Dame.[99] The Cubs now had another young college pitcher to go along with cold-weather specialist Carl Lundgren, signed out of the University of Illinois a few years before.

But Selee never got to see how the Cubs finished in 1905, nor did he ever win a pennant with the team, because 90 games into the 1905 season, Selee became incurably ill with tuberculosis. He was given an indefinite leave of absence; he did not manage again.[100] He did, however, leave an impressive legacy. He had been a lead architect of the 116-win 1906 Cubs team—the winningest Major League Baseball team of the twentieth century. Moreover, his youth movement formed the foundation on which the 1906–10 Cubs dynasty was built.[101] Selee's legacy was validated when, in 1999, he was elected to the National Baseball Hall of Fame.[102]

////

Following Selee's departure in 1905, Frank Chance was named as Selee's replacement. Some accounts say that owner Hart picked Chance for the job. Other accounts say that Hart allowed the players to select their manager— equivalent to letting inmates choose their own warden. In any event, Chance became the player-manager. When Chance took over in 1905, the Cubs were in fourth place, but under him, they finished the season winning 40 and losing only 23.[103] With this season-ending run, the Cubs finished at 92-61, in third place, 13 games behind the first-place New York Giants.

The 1905 team, however, while improved with good pitching, still lacked a potent offense. There was also internal strife. On September 14, Johnny Evers had an on-field fistfight with shortstop Joe Tinker. Even though the two would play side by side for years and eventually become immortalized together, the fight left Tinker and Evers on nonspeaking terms for years. "Tinker and myself hated each other, but we loved the Cubs," said Evers years later. "We wouldn't fight for each other, but we'd come close to killing people for our team. That was one of the answers to the Cubs success."[104]

To cap off a 1905 season that featured some bumps in the road but saw continuing improvement, the Cubs beat the White Sox in their annual postseason City Series. This was a popular exhibition between Chicago's two big-league teams held at the same time as the World Series.[105] Throughout the 1906 season, the Cubs flew a pennant beyond the center-field fence at West Side Grounds to boast of their 1905 City Series victory over the Sox.

The Cubs Rebuild, Step 2: Acquiring Veterans

After the third-place finish in 1905, and with the youth movement showing promise, Chance began to implement the next step of the rebuilding process. Chance knew that if he could patch a few holes, the Cubs could contend for a title. He felt that the team needed a third baseman and a hard-hitting outfielder, as well as some additional pitching. Chance was then given authority by new Cubs president Charles Murphy to obtain proven players.

One obstacle was that Chance was precluded from going after veterans from other big-league clubs by the ubiquitous reserve clause. Therefore, in trying to add seasoned veterans to the youthful lineup the Cubs had already

assembled, Chance's only option was to engage in trades. During the 1905–6 offseason, Chance capitalized on his trade opportunities.

First, Chance learned from his close player contacts that outfielder Jimmy Sheckard was unhappy as a member of the Brooklyn Superbas (later known as the Dodgers). This insight allowed the Cubs to work a trade with Brooklyn, and on December 30, 1905, Chicago acquired the hard-hitting outfielder.[106] Sheckard would patrol left field for the team. A good hitter, he had previously led the National League in home runs and triples, and blessed with good speed, he twice led the league in stolen bases.[107]

Sheckard had two qualities that Chance especially valued: toughness and speed. He could also be entertaining, pulling off comic routines with center fielder and super-sub Artie "Sol" Hofman, such as a game of tag, for the

Opposite: Cubs left-fielder Jimmy Sheckard. *Chicago History Museum*.

Left: Cubs third baseman Harry Steinfeldt. *Chicago History Museum*.

amusement of the fans. Sheckard was respected as a teammate and played the role of team leader when Chance was absent.[108]

In March 1906, the Cubs were able to trade for another veteran, third baseman Harry Steinfeldt. He had established himself as a good fielder and would lead the Cubs in hitting in 1906. In later years, "Harry Steinfeldt" would be the answer to an often-asked trivia question: "Who was the third baseman who played alongside Tinker, Evers and Chance?"

That same 1905–6 offseason, Chance was able to acquire the additional pitching he sought by obtaining starting southpaw Jack Pfiester from the Pirates. Pfiester would later pitch some of the biggest games in Cubs history. He would earn the nickname "Giant Killer" after the Cubs shellacked New York, 19–0, in 1906 with Pfiester on the hill.

In managing the club to a fast finish at the end of the 1905 season and then adding proven veterans in the offseason, Chance demonstrated his outstanding leadership skills. Furthermore, while he was "gruff" and "stern" on the field, "after the day's work" was done he relaxed with the boys and enjoyed their company.[109] He did not "carry anger or criticism off the field with him," which was "a big reason" the players liked him, were "proud of him" and would "work their heads off for him"—all signs of a great leader.[110] Chance's leadership skills inspired Charles Dryden, a legendary *Chicago Tribune* sportswriter, to call him the "Peerless Leader," a title by which Chance would forever be known.[111]

PART III
1906

Chapter 1

SPRING 1906

The Jungle *and the San Francisco Earthquake*
Overshadow Preseason Baseball Hopes

Down every side street they could see, it was…always the same endless vista of
ugly and dirty little wooden buildings. Here and there would be a bridge crossing
a filthy creek, with hard-baked mud shores and dingy sheds and docks along it.
—Upton Sinclair, describing Chicago in The Jungle, *1906*[112]

In the early 1900s, working conditions for the average Chicagoan were
grueling and grim. But conditions in the meatpacking plants of the South
Side Stockyards were unbearable. A young socialist from New Jersey named
Upton Sinclair came to Chicago to investigate. As part of his investigation, he
visited with, and heard stories from, immigrant workers of their unbearable
working conditions, desolate surroundings, crushing poverty and overall
hopelessness, all foisted on them by privileged and wealthy business investors.
Sinclair also meandered through the putrid, dangerous working areas of the
stockyards and meatpacking plants, witnessing how pieces of meat lying in
human spit on filthy floors overrun by rodents would be retrieved for later
sale and public consumption.[113]

In February 1906, Sinclair began making headlines with his best-selling
novel *The Jungle*, which depicted the working conditions and unsanitary
practices of the Chicago stockyards and meatpacking industry.[114] *The Jungle*
tells the story of a fictional immigrant family arriving in Chicago, unable
to speak English, with no money or skills and initially not knowing what to

do or where to go. The novel contains heartbreaking passages of suffering and abuse. In one passage, a young boy comes in from the bitter cold with his ears so frozen that in minutes they break off short. The terrible working conditions and exploitation of workers detailed in the book sparked outrage across the country. The book also found a fan in the White House.

Like Sinclair, President Theodore Roosevelt deplored the special benefits held by the "privileged few." Following Sinclair's novel, Roosevelt appointed a commission to investigate. The commissioners found that Sinclair's claims were substantially true. As a result, Roosevelt returned to Chicago in June 1906 to take action. After inspecting the stockyards and packinghouses, the president expressed the dire need for change, not only in the working conditions but also regarding the unsanitary handling of food product. According to the *Chicago Daily News* of June 4, 1906, President Roosevelt said: "The conditions shown by even this short inspection to exist in the Chicago stockyards are revolting. It is imperatively necessary in the interest of decency that they should be radically changed. The report shows that the stockyards and packing houses are not even reasonably clean and that the method of handling food products is uncleanly and dangerous to health."

Encouraged by the president, on June 30, 1906, Congress passed the Federal Meat Inspection Act of 1906. It prevented unhealthy meat and meat products from being sold as food and ensured that meat and meat products are processed under sanitary conditions. That same day, the Pure Food and Drug Act was also passed, protecting the general population from unhealthy and fraudulently misrepresented food products.[115]

###

While Sinclair's book was jumping off bookshelves in the spring of 1906, new Cubs owner Charles W. Murphy took over as team president just prior to the beginning of the season. But Murphy was not the only new feature on the Chicago baseball scene, as new and improved versions of both the Cubs and the White Sox were being unveiled for the upcoming season.

During spring training, Chance's beliefs that newly acquired veterans could transform the Cubs into contenders were bolstered by his preseason observations. After seeing newly acquired pitcher Jack Pfiester throw well in an exhibition, Chance predicted that he would be a helpful addition to the pitching staff.[116] Chance also noted that recently acquired third baseman

Harry Steinfeldt had "rounded out the infield," was exhibiting good defense and was "hitting the ball a mile."[117] Furthermore, Chance observed that hard-hitting, speedy outfielder Jimmy Sheckard, who had been acquired from Brooklyn, was "happy to be with a fast team."[118]

President Charlie Murphy echoed Chance's observations, boasting after a preseason series in Indianapolis that the pitching was so deep that Chance would have a hard time deciding which pitchers to use. Murphy also summed up the Cubs' prospects by saying, "The team looks strong in every department."[119] That would later prove to be an understatement.

Going into the 1906 regular season, the Cubs had the following lineup:

Jimmy Slagle, CF
Jimmy Sheckard, LF
Frank Schulte, RF
Frank Chance, 1B
Harry Steinfeldt, 3B
Joe Tinker, SS
Johnny Evers, 2B
Johnny Kling, C
Pitcher

When the 1906 season got underway, Frank Chance and his Cubs had reasonably high expectations for success. But it is unlikely that, in their wildest dreams, they could have foreseen the succession of invincible summers to come.

////

On Chicago's South Side, the approach of the 1906 preseason brought with it reasonably high expectations as well. The White Sox had finished in second place in the American League in 1905 and appeared to offer the greatest pennant threat to the defending champion Philadelphia Athletics. The Sox were led by their center fielder and player-manager, Fielder Jones ("Fielder" was his actual given first name); their shortstop, future Hall of Famer George Davis; and a stalwart pitching staff featuring Nick Altrock and another future Hall of Famer, veteran spitball artist Eddie Walsh. They played their home games at Thirty-Ninth and Wentworth, not far from the stockyards and meatpacking plants.

Despite high preseason expectations, the time leading up to the start of the 1906 season did not go particularly well for the Sox. First, in the offseason, one of their top pitchers, Jimmy Callahan, left the team to become co-owner of the semipro Logan Squares. Later, Sox spring training was marred by rainout after rainout. On April 5 in Nashville, after yet another rainout, Sox management fretted that the team had been idle for so long that the players would be in poor condition, susceptible to sore arms and other maladies.[120] Management's concerns about the stamina and conditioning of the Sox players would turn out to be well-founded.

On April 17, the 1906 White Sox, who would become known to posterity as the "Hitless Wonders," opened their season with an uncharacteristically big day offensively, beating the Tigers. That same day, the Cubs (having opened the season five days earlier than the Sox and gone 3-2 in Cincinnati) did not do as well in their home opener, falling to the St. Louis Cardinals.

The next day, while Chicagoans were enjoying the arrival of spring weather and the start of the baseball season, a tragic event was unfolding two thousand miles away. The event would result in massive human suffering and, despite occurring far away, have a substantial impact on the city of Chicago. It would even directly touch the Cubs.

////

On April 18, 1906, a powerful earthquake ripped through San Francisco, causing skyscrapers to come tumbling down. When they did, gas pipes broke, electric wires became crossed and water became unavailable. This led to a wild and devastating fire that raged through the city for three days, creating terror in the streets. Eight square miles of the city were destroyed, and in that area, few shops remained standing. Nearly all buildings at Stanford University in faraway Palo Alto were destroyed. The death toll from the earthquake and subsequent fire was approximately three thousand, with thousands more injured or displaced.[121]

Survivors who escaped the earthquake and fire and were able to return by train to Chicago told of the horrors they experienced. Some told of waking in their hotel beds with the walls rumbling. Their hotel seemed on the verge of collapse, with loose plaster flying across the room. Others spoke of their first impressions on leaving their hotels: dead bodies on the street, having been crushed by building walls, and fires lighting up the street. A pastor told of staying with friends in a house on the outskirts

Meeting of Chicagoans involved in San Francisco earthquake relief. *Chicago History Museum.*

of the city when they heard a sound like a thunderstorm followed by the building beginning to sway. The pastor and his friends scrambled to escape the house just prior to its collapsing.[122]

Chicagoans, many of whom recalled the generosity received from outsiders after the Great Fire of 1871, responded in kind to the plight of the citizens of San Francisco. Hundreds of organizations, agencies and churches and thousands of individual Chicagoans made rushing funds and aid to beleaguered San Francisco a top priority. Hundreds of thousands of dollars—a huge amount in those days—was raised from the coffers of Chicagoans. According to anecdotal evidence, even those with few assets gave what they could to aid their brothers and sisters on the West Coast.[123]

One San Francisco native who suffered mightily from the earthquake was Cal McVey, a former member of the Cubs' West Coast scouting network, which years before had discovered Frank Chance and recommended him to the team. McVey, who by 1906 was out of the game and owned a cigar store, not only lost his home and his business from the quake, but his wife was seriously injured as well. After the earthquake, McVey was relegated to living in a shack. When word of his plight reached the Cubs organization, they responded like family.[124] A fund was established for McVey's benefit, with Cap Anson as treasurer. Sporting-goods magnate and former Cubs legend Albert Spalding was the first to contribute, and when the team was thrown a season-ending banquet, funds left over from the event were donated to the McVey fund.

※※※

In attempting to rebuild its city, the San Francisco Merchants Association, headed by former mayor James Phelan, asked a noted Chicagoan for help. Daniel Burnham was known nationally for his work on the White City and projects in Washington, D.C., and Manila. He had also done some work for San Francisco.

Burnham traveled to San Francisco to work on a city rebuilding plan. Most of its citizens understandably wanted the city rebuilt quickly, inexpensively and just the way it had been. They were not looking for grandiose, high-priced improvements. Burnham came up with a modest plan that he felt addressed those concerns, and on May 21, the San Francisco Board of Supervisors approved Burnham's plan. Burnham then returned by train to Chicago.[125] What he did not know on his ride back to Chicago was that, without him remaining in San Francisco to persuade and push through his modest plan, it died and was never implemented.

On the other hand, Burnham's return train trip to Chicago led to a different engagement for him that would have grandiose designs and profound implications for the city of Chicago.

※※※

While on the train, Burnham had occasion to meet and speak with Joseph Medill McCormick, the publisher of the *Chicago Tribune*. During that meeting, McCormick broached the subject of Burnham doing a plan for his hometown.[126] Civic pride was a substantial motivation for McCormick in seeking out Burnham. In truth, the city's reputation had taken a substantial hit after the publication in 1904 of Lincoln Steffens's *The Shame of the Cities* and then Upton Sinclair's *The Jungle* two years later.[127] McCormick believed that a grand plan and vision for the city was necessary to counteract the less-than-stellar image that Chicago had been developing.

To Burnham, McCormick's suggestion of a city plan for Chicago was nothing new. Burnham had long believed that something needed to be done to overcome the many obstacles, especially congestion and pollution,[128] preventing Chicago from reaching its full potential. McCormick's suggestion that Burnham devise a plan would have been gratifying for Burnham to hear, but Burnham was leery, believing that the city's commercial interests would balk at the plan. After returning to Chicago, McCormick took up the issue with the city's commercial interests, as represented by the Commercial Club of Chicago and the Merchants Club of Chicago.

The Merchants Club was a group of very successful local businessmen. They tended to be younger and more progressive than their older and wealthier counterparts in the Commercial Club. But both clubs shared a common interest in promoting the city of Chicago. Many members of both groups shared positions on prominent civic, business, professional and philanthropic boards and knew one another from dealings outside of their clubs. They were a very "tight-knit and like-minded group."[129]

The members of the Merchants Club were very much aware that early twentieth-century Chicago was not only dirty and aesthetically challenged but also manifested "the chaos incident to rapid growth, and especially to the influx of people of many nationalities without common traditions or habits of life."[130] More so than the conservative Commercial Club, the Merchants Club believed that it was time for the city to bring order out of such chaos and turn it into a far more livable place. While the Merchants Club originally took the lead in promoting a plan, the Merchants Club and Commercial Club later merged to create one. To put together a new city plan to make their vision a reality, they saw Burnham as their man. They were aware of his planning efforts for San Francisco and other cities, and of course they were aware of his spectacular White City. He had even designed the downtown buildings in which many of the Merchants Club and Commercial Club members had offices. Not insignificantly, Burnham had also demonstrated the ability to not only impart beauty and culture into his architecture but also create architecture that would serve business interests and produce profits for his clients.

Representatives of the Merchants Club of Chicago and the Commercial Club, at the behest of McCormick, began discussions with Burnham concerning the possibility of putting together a plan for Chicago that would gain acceptance throughout the city.[131] The plan that would eventually emerge in 1909 would have a profound impact on the Chicago lakefront and other parts of the city.

Chapter 2

SUMMER 1906

Chicago Baseball Sizzles and a City Plan Takes Shape

He [Sox pitcher Ed Walsh] *threw a spitball—I think it would disintegrate
on its way to the plate and the catcher put it back together again.
I swear, when it went past the plate it was just the spit that went by.*
—*Detroit's "Wahoo" Sam Crawford*[132]

While the summer of 1906 saw Burnham and the city's commercial
elite engaged in discussions concerning a historic City Plan, the 1906
Cubs and White Sox were both on their way to making history of their own.

By May, around the time that Burnham was traveling to and from San
Francisco after the earthquake, the Cubs had moved into first place for the
first time since 1901. Fans were "in a joyous mood, not only because the
Cubs were in first place, but also because they had supplanted the despised
defending world champion New York Giants," whose "win by any means"
refrain rubbed Chicagoans the wrong way.[133]

Despite their early season success in 1906, the Cubs were not content to
stand pat. In early June, while San Francisco was trying to rebuild, Frank
Chance was continuing his own rebuilding efforts. Chance got a bargain
in a deal with Cincinnati, obtaining starting pitcher Orval Overall, whom
Chance had known back in California. At six feet, two inches tall and
over two hundred pounds, Overall was a big man for his day. The June 4,
1906 issue of the *Chicago Daily News* remarked: "Chance could not find a
uniform big enough for the Californian [Overall], except for [trainer] Jack
McCormick's, so the trainer was deprived of his clothes and will have to
keep off the bench until he can get a new one."

Shortly after, on June 7, the Cubs faced Giants ace and future Hall of Famer Christy Mathewson, who would eventually be considered one of the greatest pitchers of all time. Mathewson was a dominating pitcher with uncanny control, once going sixty-eight innings without issuing a walk.

Not only was Mathewson a "control" pitcher, but he also valued self-control as a critical standard in living his life. "Matty" was a genuinely fine human being, a gentleman at a time when most ballplayers were crude and rough-edged. According to teammate Fred Snodgrass, he was "a wonderful man, reserved, but when you got to know him, just a truly good friend."[134] Mathewson was the kind of fellow most guys could emulate: tall, good-looking, athletic, college-educated (Bucknell), smart (straight-A student), classy and good at just about everything he tried. He excelled at golf, billiards and poker. He was also a checkers champion in several states, known to be able to play three opponents at one time and beat every one of them. With all his exemplary attributes, parents and teachers held Mathewson up as a role model. In the early twentieth century, Mathewson was considered the face of baseball.[135]

On that June day, facing the great Mathewson promised to be no easy task, but the Cubs were up to the challenge. They pounded Mathewson and his successor, Joe "Iron Man" McGinty, for 11 runs in the first inning, with Mathewson knocked out and sent to the earliest shower of his great career. In the meantime, Jack Pfiester hurled a shutout for the Cubs, and Chicago humiliated the Giants, 19–0. The blowout earned Pfiester the title "Jack the Giant Killer."[136]

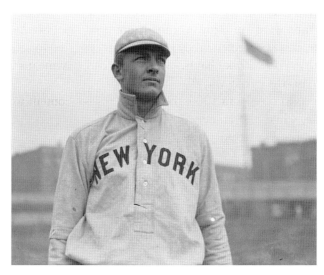

New York Giants pitcher Christy Mathewson. *Chicago History Museum.*

By July 22, 1906, the Cubs had a commanding lead in the National League, and the prevailing mood in Chicago was that the team had all but wrapped up the pennant.[137] The Cubs, however, were just getting on a roll. During a 39-game stretch from August 6 to September 18, they had a 37-2 record. During that stretch, they won 11 games in a row, lost 1 game, won 14 in a row, lost 1 game and then won 12 in a row.

All in all, the 1906 Cubs played only 152 of their 154 regularly scheduled games. Two of their games were postponed but never played, yet they won an astonishing 116 and lost only 36, a winning percentage of .763—a mark that has never been equaled. Had the Cubs been allowed to play their full complement of 154 games, they could have won 118 games. Their record of 116 victories was matched only once, by the 2001 Seattle Mariners. But the Mariners were able to accomplish that feat in the era of a 162-game season. As it was, the 1906 Cubs left the defending NL champion Giants 20 games behind.[138]

In 1906, catcher Johnny Kling enjoyed his best season at the plate with a .312 average, fifteen doubles, eight triples and two home runs in 107 games. Steinfeldt led the team in hitting, batting .327 with three home runs and eighty-three RBIs.[139]

Most instrumental, however, in their tremendous success that year was the Cubs' pitching, even better than in 1905. Brown was nearly unhittable, with a 26-6 record and a miniscule 1.04 ERA. He captured the NL's MVP award. Reulbach was nearly as spectacular, with a 19-4 record and a 1.65 ERA.[140] Pfiester won 20 games for the only time in his career, with a 1.51 ERA; and the Illini alumnus Lundgren finished at 17-6.

The Cubs were so far ahead of the pack that they clinched the pennant on September 19, weeks before the season ended. The next day, huge Cub fan "Bathhouse" Coughlin took an awkward stab at summarizing the season with another one of his silly poems:

Sept 20, 1906
Chicago Record Herald
Ballad of the Flag
FIRST INNING.
Come, gather round me, baseball fans, while I a tale unfold
Of how Chicago won the flag, the first since days of old,
With Chance, our gallant captain, and his crew of sprightly cubs
We made the other league teams look like Indians dubs.[141]

Coughlin's inane poem continued to drone on, and for some reason continued through the eleventh "inning." The final ten "innings" of Coughlin's poem are not shown here to spare the reader.

In any event, having captured the pennant so early, the confident Cubs had plenty of time to savor their success and contemplate drubbing whatever "champion" the upstart American League would offer up as a sacrifice in the World Series.

////

In the early part of the 1906 season, the White Sox were plagued by injuries, possibly as a result of all the spring training rainouts impeding their physical conditioning. Shortstop George Davis and catcher Billy Sullivan missed considerable early season playing time. Reflecting their numerous injuries, in mid-May, the Sox were buried in seventh place, and by June, they were still mired in the second division, occupying sixth place.

In June, however, the Sox hired "Doc" Conibear as their strength and conditioning coach. Doc's training programs revitalized the team. By August, they had climbed to fourth place. Then they went on a tear, including a nineteen-game winning streak late in the season, putting them in position to take the pennant.[142]

The rise of the 1906 White Sox was certainly not a result of any hitting prowess. They finished the season with a team batting average of just .228 and had no .300 hitters. Second baseman and future Hall of Famer Frank "the Bald Eagle" Isbell led the team in hitting with a .279 average. Third baseman Lee Tannehill hit an anemic .183. Collectively, the weak-hitting White Sox became known as the "Hitless Wonders" because, despite a lack of offense, they were still able to win. The Sox had mastered the "inside game," in which bunts, sacrifices, steals and hit-and-runs were used to manufacture runs.

In addition, the Sox boasted a talented pitching staff led by veteran spit-baller and future Hall of Famer Eddie Walsh. Eddie was the youngest of thirteen children who often gathered with their mother to sing Irish folk songs at home. But he grew to become very cocky, and it was said of Walsh that he could strut while standing still.[143] His pitching performances, however, could back up his swagger.

In 1906, Walsh had a record of 17-13 with a sparkling 1.88 earned run average, and his spitball was one of the most effective pitches in baseball.

Batters, accustomed to facing fastballs and curves, found his "spitter" befuddling. At times, his spitball would drop two feet or move two feet away.[144] Walter Johnson called Walsh's delivery "about the most tantalizing in baseball" for the way the ball arrived at the plate "with such terrific speed, and unerringly dives just as if it knew what it was about and tried to dodge the hitter's bat."[145]

If a batter was able to reach first base, he would find that Walsh's move to first was as good as anyone's. Many picked-off base runners complained that Walsh's move constituted a balk, or at least "half a balk." Eventually inducted into the National Baseball Hall of Fame, Walsh today still holds the major league career ERA record of 1.82.

Walsh was not the only star in the Sox's starting rotation in 1906. Frank Owens and Nick Altrock were both 20-game winners. Owens led the staff in victories with a 22-13 record, and Altrock finished with a 20-13 record and an impressive 2.06 ERA. The team's ERA leader, Doc White (1.52), had an 18-6 record.

White Sox pitcher Ed Walsh. *Chicago History Museum.*

During August and September, the Sox and New York Highlanders traded first- and second-place positions several times. The Sox, however, started to pull away in late September.

On October 3, 1906, the Sox, who were rained out in St. Louis, knew that if the Philadelphia Athletics could win one of the two games that day in their doubleheader against New York, Chicago would clinch the pennant. The Sox players went down to the local newspaper office, where they focused on the outside bulletin board, which displayed updates on the New York–Philadelphia doubleheader. When the board showed that the Athletics had won the second game, eliminating New York and clinching a pennant for the White Sox, the Chicago players "danced, howled, and cavorted like maniacs" while drenched in the rain.[146] A crowd gathered around and joined the players, and they all danced and yelled until dark. So loud did they howl that police arrived on the scene, thinking that a riot might be taking place. The police tried to restrain the jubilant Sox, but "they might as well have ordered the rain to stop."[147] Later, the players continued the celebration in their hotel lobby, where they were spotted doing somersaults, more dancing and even a little "ring around the rosy" in pure joy.

After the Sox clinched the pennant, the *Tribune*'s Hugh Fullerton reported: "Last night Chicago was baseball mad. Men stood and cheered in elevated trains when the news was passed along that the Sox were safe and that Chicago had two pennants—and the world championship."[148] The Cubs and Sox were both going to the World Series!

Chapter 3

FALL 1906

The World Series

A civil war.
—Tribune*'s Charles Dryden*

The 1906 World Series was scheduled to start on October 9. Coincidentally, that was "Chicago Day," the day commemorating the thirty-fifth anniversary of the Great Fire of 1871. The Cubs, winners of 116 games, were heavily favored over the Hitless Wonders, who had won only 93 games. But in anticipation of the upcoming World Series, fans of both teams strutted and bragged.

On the day of the series opener, the *Chicago Daily News* trumpeted, "Chicago Seized by a Baseball Frenzy."[149] The *Tribune*'s Charles Dryden likened the World Series to a "civil war."[150] Fans were said to be "baseball mad" and "in full blast."[151] Even women were said to be "enthusiastic."[152] The Chicago Board of Trade quit work at 1:20 p.m. to allow traders to get to the ballpark. Some city workers had a shortened day as well. Bathhouse Coughlin said, "Sure, close up the City Hall and give the boys a chance to see the game."[153]

The *Daily News* reported the efforts of some to get the afternoon off from work: "Sporting circles and places where the fans want to congregate became congested before the hour of the game and when the holders of almost priceless tickets to the World's Series departed, every office boy and clerk had slain his grandmother or some near relative and the funeral was held at the park. Stomach aches were frequent."[154]

On downtown streets, arguments between partisans of the two fan bases were continual, and on occasion fists were raised. Throughout the city, little work was getting done, except for the police, who were busy making hundreds of arrests of fighting Cubs and Sox fans.[155] A newspaper foreman felt the need to separate his employees, sending all the Sox fans to one area and the Cub fans to another to minimize disruption and to get the paper printed on time.[156] The fans "simply raged all over the Loop district. Hustling, bustling mobs pushed themselves onward to catch trains for the park and those who drew the almost fatal order from their employers that there would be no holidays this afternoon kept the wires hot with inquiries as to the scores."[157]

The World Series consumed the minds and time of nearly all the city's inhabitants. One of the papers sent out reporters to try to find any male who was not aware that the Cubs and Sox were playing in the championship. After several days of searching, only one man, a German butcher, was found to have no knowledge of baseball or of the upcoming World Series.[158]

Most impartial observers saw the Cubs as clear favorites. They saw how the Cubs ran roughshod over the rest of the National League during the regular season and recalled how the team had manhandled the Sox in the 1905 season-ending City Series.

One analytical and impartial observer, however, defied conventional wisdom and predicted a Sox victory in six games. Originally, the *Chicago Tribune*'s Hugh Fullerton expected a Cubs victory. But he looked at several factors that he believed would break in favor of the Sox. For one, the great crowds would force the insertion of additional seating in both left and right fields. The restricted outfield space that resulted would negate any advantage held by the Cubs' better-fielding left and right fielders, Schulte and Sheckard. Furthermore, according to Fullerton, center field would not be obstructed with additional seating, thus posing no hindrance to the superior defensive skills of Sox center fielder Jones, whom Fullerton believed was superior defensively to Cubs center fielder Slagle. Fullerton also believed that the superior defensive skills of Sox pitchers and their consistency in being able to cover first base gave Sox first baseman Jiggs Donohue more "leeway." Fullerton also gave the Sox infield the defensive edge over their West Side counterparts.[159]

Fullerton also counted on the Sox winning "the inside game." He believed that Sox owner Charles Comiskey "knew more baseball than any two men." He also believed that Jones, Davis, Isbell and Sullivan had the experience and know-how to tutor less-experienced players to win at "inside ball." Fullerton was especially impressed with how the Hitless

Wonders were able to "score more runs on fewer hits." For example, he believed that Cubs pitcher Mordecai Brown would prove difficult for the Sox to hit, but with the Sox perfecting their use of the inside game, they would nonetheless beat Brown.

Fullerton was also somewhat dismissive of the Cubs' supposed hitting superiority, believing that NL pitching was not as challenging as that in the AL. He also believed that the South Side crowds were more partisan than those on the West Side and would give the Sox the advantage there. All in all, Fullerton defied the oddsmakers and other so-called experts. He picked the Sox to triumph in six games.[160] His prediction would prove accurate.

More important, Sox manager Fielder Jones was a believer in his team's chances. He knew that during the regular season American League fans had shown little respect for the Sox. Speaking prior to the series of those AL naysayers, however, Jones asserted that "some are weak-kneed because the Cubs beat us in last year's post-series. The statistics of those games show that we made more runs off Cubs pitchers than we did in any series before or since. Then our pitchers were in miserable shape, but now all my boxmen are fit and ready. We have had much to contend with this season, but things at last are beginning to break better, and I believe we will surely win the World's Championship."[161]

⁄⁄⁄⁄

Frigid temperatures coupled with nasty winds greeted those fans willing to venture out to the Cubs' West Side Grounds on October 9, 1906, to see Game One of the World Series. The overcast, arctic-like weather was more suitable for football than baseball. Pregame flurries gave way to actual snowfall during the second inning. Just the day before, the weather had been beautiful, which made the cold feel even more unbearable.[162] In any event, thousands lined up outside the ballpark well before the gates opened at noon, wearing fur coats, buffalo robes, rugs and heavy winter overcoats.[163]

West Side Grounds was a two-tiered wooden stadium located near the present site of the University of Illinois Medical Center on the near West Side. The home of the Cubs since 1892, West Side Grounds seated thirteen thousand. Its high wooden outfield walls were covered with brightly colored advertisements for local businesses. Its dimensions, unlike today's ballparks, were not conducive to home runs. While the distance from home to the left-field wall was a reachable 340 feet and the distance to right field only 316 feet, the distance to left center jumped to 441 feet, the distance to center field was 475 feet and the distance to the center-field corner was a mammoth 520 feet.[164] Beyond the left-field wall was a mental institution, from which inmates might occasionally and unexpectedly wander over to the ballpark. From that scenario came the expression, "It came out of left field."

For Game One of the World Series, the park was decked out with American flags and red, white and blue bunting, befitting a special occasion. Meanwhile, in deep center field, the same large white "pennant" flag that the Cubs had won from the Sox following the 1905 postseason City Series was raised. The Sox were determined to take that flag back.[165]

Cubs owner Charles Murphy anticipated a crowd of more than twenty-five thousand and had boosted stadium capacity by placing some six thousand "circus" seats in the outfield, roped off from the rest of the playing field and resulting in new ground rules. Due to the weather, however, only thirteen thousand fans attended.

In those days, fans who could not get to the ballpark usually followed the daily exploits of their team in the local newspaper. But for this World Series, much of the populace demanded more immediate information than a newspaper could provide. As a result, the *Tribune* arranged for up-to-the-minute information such as the score, inning, number of outs and men on base to be carried over telegraph lines to the Auditorium and First Regent Armory, where the game was effectively re-created indoors on large "scoreboards" for the crowds inside. Nine thousand fans gathered in the warmer environs of the Auditorium and First Regent Armory to follow the progress.[166]

Back at West Side Grounds, ticket prices were double what they were in the regular season. Bleacher seats now cost $0.50, grandstand tickets went for $1.00 or $1.50 and boxes were $2.00. Scalpers were asking anywhere from two to ten times face value for tickets. It was hoped that the $0.50 bleacher prices would "improve the morale of the crowd"[167] and curtail the usual throwing of pop bottles from the bleachers. In those days, the throwing of pop bottles by fans either irate or drunk—or both—was a matter of considerable concern. The umpires were the regular targets of the throwers, but the players occasionally found themselves marked men as well. Even fans found themselves in the line of fire. Chicago cops, both in uniform and plain clothes, were in the crowd to arrest anyone who dared to throw a bottle.[168]

Game time was set for 2:30 p.m., a half hour earlier than usual, to allow for more daylight as the October days grew shorter. Many ballparks had no facilities for the visiting team to dress, so visitors rode from the hotel to the ballpark through the city's streets in an open horse-drawn wagon, sometimes called a "tallyho," in full uniform. The wagons customarily attracted the attention of local kids, and on occasion people on the sidewalks would not exactly act as gracious hosts. It was not uncommon for the visitors siting in the open wagons to have rotten tomatoes hurled at them.[169]

As was customary for the times, it was agreed that, for this series, the visiting team would dress for the game in a downtown hotel and travel in full uniform to the ballpark. Therefore, for the series opener, the visiting White Sox gathered at noon at the Victoria Hotel downtown, where they donned their playing "spangles." The team then boarded a caravan of horse-drawn carriages to take them through the business district and near West Side neighborhoods, navigating train tracks and competing for space on the busy streets with wagons and other vehicles. As the horse-drawn caravan moved through the streets, the Sox players in their uniforms were easily recognized by the crowds, who greeted them warmly with shouts and cheers all along their route.[170] There were no reports of "rotten tomatoes" being thrown at the AL champs. Perhaps arrogant Cubs fans had so little respect for the underdog Sox that they were not deemed worth harassing.

Both teams entered the World Series somewhat affected by injuries. For the Sox, veteran shortstop George Davis would not be ready to go in the opener. Good-hitting but poor-fielding George Rohe would take his place, filling in at third while Tannehill moved from third to short. Sox catcher Sullivan had been nursing a sore thumb on his throwing hand but would be able to go.

For the Cubs, center fielder Jimmy Slagle was suffering from a severe chest bruise and was replaced by Artie "Sol" Hofman. Ace pitcher Mordecai Brown was nursing a sore arm he had developed at the end of the regular season. In fact, there was speculation that Brown would not be ready to go for the opener and that Ed Reulbach would get the nod for the West Siders. But Brown declared that he was ready, and Chance decided to go with his ace.

To oppose Brown, Sox manager Fielder Jones had the option of going with Nick Altrock, veteran Eddie Walsh or Doc White as his opening game starting pitcher.[171] Jones went with Altrock, who was the only Sox hurler to have beaten the Cubs in the previous year's postseason series.[172]

White Sox player-manager Fielder Jones. *Chicago History Museum.*

The game was scoreless through the first four innings. In the top of the fifth, the Sox's replacement third baseman, George Rohe, ripped a shot past third base down the left-field line. Normally, this would have resulted in a double. But while trying to retrieve the ball, left fielder Jimmy Sheckard inadvertently kicked it under the ropes and into the temporary field-seating area. According to the ground rules put in place for the World Series games played at West Side Park, this resulted in a ground-rule triple.[173]

One out later, with Rohe still at third, right fielder Patsy Dougherty dribbled a roller just to the left of the plate. Brown pounced on it and quickly fired to catcher Kling well in advance of the sliding Rohe. But the usually reliable Kling dropped the throw, and the Sox had the first lead of the game, 1–0.[174]

In the top of the sixth, Brown walked the lead-off man, pitcher Altrock. It is often the case that when a pitcher walks his opposing counterpart—especially if the opposing pitcher is leading off an inning—dire consequences will follow. The next batter, Hahn, laid down a sacrifice bunt, moving Altrock to second. Altrock was later thrown out at the plate trying to score on a single by Jones, but Jones scored the Sox's second run on a soft single by Isbell. Sox 2, Cubs 0.

The Cubs got a run in their half of the sixth on a wild pitch, making the score 2–1, but that is all they would score that day. The Cubs got a hit in each of the eighth and ninth innings, but in the ninth, when Steinfeldt's fly to center was caught by Jones, the Sox center fielder jumped in the air and waved his hand over his head in celebration. The White Sox had an improbable Game One victory over the heavily favored Cubs.[175]

Sox fans have always had a reputation as a generally rowdy bunch, but back then, they took rowdiness to a different level. For example, it was not uncommon for them to take to the field and attack the umpire. They reflected the team's rough-and-tumble Bridgeport neighborhood.[176] So, with the White Sox having vanquished the Cubs in Game One of the World Series, hundreds, if not thousands, of delirious supporters stormed the field. This time, however, they carried White Sox players—especially Altrock and Rohe—on their shoulders while police officers tried to offer some protection to the two Sox heroes.

While their supporters were exuberant, the Sox players and management seemed unfazed by their victory. "I was not surprised by the result," said Manager Jones after the game. "I don't know whether Davis will be able to play tomorrow or not. Does it make any difference? We have played along without star men all season and have kept right on winning. It seems to be our luck to have everything break right for us when it looks darkest."[177]

Early the next day, Nick Altrock appeared to echo his manager's statement. In fact, he sounded as if he had not been very impressed with the Cubs. "They were easier than that St. Louis bunch a week ago Monday….The cold weather did not seem to affect me yesterday at all. They should have been shut out, except for that wild pitch. The ball was a little wet and it slipped. We will give them another dose today on the South Side."[178]

∅∅∅

While the venue for Game Two, South Side Park, was different than that of the day before, the weather was much the same. A brisk wind blowing from the lake easily tossed the light snowflakes that fell at game time. The temperature hovered around freezing, but the wind made it feel much colder. The players came out wearing sweaters and would continue to wear them, even during the game.[179]

The cold, however, did not dampen the spirits of the fans. The Chicago Board of Trade sent a huge delegation to the game, and as was the case before the first game, many workers in the city found ways to escape the office or factory by 1:00 p.m. On the streets, taunting and arguments between fans of the opposing teams were common. Nonetheless, attendance for Game Two at South Side Park was a disappointing 12,692, close to the attendance for Game One at West Side Grounds. When the Sox took the field for pregame practice, Rohe, the hitting star of Game One, was given a rousing ovation by Sox fans, and when Altrock took the field, the crowd went wild.[180]

Most observers assumed that the Cubs would start their cold-weather master, Carl Lundgren, given the frigid conditions. But Chance decided to go with ex–Notre Damer Ed Reulbach. Sox manager Fielder Jones again passed on spitball-throwing Ed Walsh, fearing that the freezing temperatures would affect his spit on the ball. Jones opted to start Doc White.[181]

Both White and Reulbach started well, each retiring the side in order in the first inning. Chance opened the Cubs' half of the second by striking out. Steinfeldt rapped a sharp single to left-center field, and Tinker laid down a perfect bunt along the third-base line. He was able to reach first without a play being made. Evers then grounded to Isbell at second for what looked to be an inning-ending double play, but Isbell chose to backhand his short throw to second, and the ball ended up in left field. Steinfeldt was able to score the first run of the game before Patsy Dougherty in left could track down the ball. Meanwhile, Tinker rambled from first to third on the play, and Evers was in safely at second.

After a visit from Jones to the mound, Kling was walked intentionally to load the bases for Reulbach. The Cubs pitcher laid down a beautiful sacrifice squeeze bunt, allowing Tinker to score the Cubs' second run. With two out, Hofman grounded to shortstop, but Tannehill, playing out of position for the second straight day due to the injury to George Davis, threw offline to first, causing Donohue to leave the base to retrieve the errant throw. Evers scored on the play.

By the end of the inning, the Cubs had a 3–0 lead. Doc White had allowed only one batted ball to leave the infield in that inning. But the White Sox defense, which had been so instrumental in Altrock's victory the day before, deserted White on this day, allowing three runs, all of which would be classified in later years as "unearned."

The Cubs added a run in the third to increase their lead to 4–0. The Sox got that run back, finally scoring in the fifth, but the Cubs scored three more times in the game.

By the bottom of the ninth, most of the crowd had left, in part due to the cold and in part due to the lopsided 7–1 score. After Sullivan flied out to center fielder Hofman to end the game, the Cubs had notched an impressive, dominating victory. The 116-win ball club that all of baseball had expected to see in the World Series had finally shown up with Reulbach's masterful, two-hit pitching and the Cubs' near-perfect execution of the inside game— hit and running, stealing bases, adept base running, sliding, bunting, hard bunting and squeezing. The team's on-field celebration was muted, however, in contrast with the wild celebration that followed the Sox victory the day before. With only a sparse crowd remaining at the end of Game Two, just a few hundred Cubs fans celebrated with players on the field.[182]

Considering the blowout win by the Cubs, the team's fans viewed the result in Game One as an aberration. After the game, Judge Kennesaw Mountain Landis, along with his fellow Cubs fans, derided the White Sox fans, saying, "What league is it your team plays in?"[183]

////

The World Series returned to West Side Grounds for Game Three. After frigid weather for the first two games, the morning of the third game brought the coldest temperature on record for that date, twenty-eight degrees. But by game time the weather had improved, and the warmth of the sun brought welcome relief.

The Armory was again packed to see the *Tribune*'s re-creation of the game. Outdoors, the warmer weather brought out a big crowd. As shown in

Sixth inning of Game Three of the 1906 World Series at West Side Grounds with Pfiester in a windup, Isbell at the plate and the bases loaded. *Chicago History Museum.*

a photo of the ballpark (above), bleachers were filled with fans ringing the outfield from foul pole to foul pole, with no break in the ring of fans in center field. Spectators jammed rooftops beyond the center-field bleachers. The Sox wore their dark jerseys and pants and white hats, and the Cubs wore light-colored uniforms.

Jack Pfiester got the Game Three starting nod from Manager Chance for the West Siders. The Sox starting pitcher was former Pennsylvania coal miner and present spitball artist Ed Walsh. Walsh had coughed up blood the morning of the game because of a cold. By late afternoon, however, as stated by the *Tribune*'s Charles Dryden, "he had the Cubs sweating blood."[184] In fact, both pitchers were in complete control for the first five innings, throwing shutout baseball.

The Cubs managed two hits in the first inning but could not score. After that, Walsh was magnificent, holding the Cubs hitless the rest of the game. They simply could never hit his spitball.

In the top half of the sixth inning of the scoreless game, weak-hitting Tannehill led off for the Sox. He singled past Steinfeldt. Walsh followed

Tannehill to the plate in an obvious bunting situation. But Pfiester pitched Walsh too finely and ended up walking the White Sox pitcher.[185] It was the second time in three games that a Cubs pitcher had walked his Sox counterpart, and like the first time, this would prove costly for the Cubs.

Hahn then came up to the plate in another obvious bunt situation. Again, Pfiester tried to foil the bunt by pitching inside to Hahn. But Pfiester's curve smacked Hahn on the side of the nose, breaking it. Hahn had to be helped off the field and taken to the hospital.[186]

The bases were now loaded with nobody out and Fielder Jones coming to the plate. Chance ordered the infield to play in close, attempting to increase the Cubs' chances of choking off the lead run at the plate. Pfiester bore down and got Jones to pop up behind the plate. Kling raced back and reached over the wires separating the field from the fans and then over the heads of the fans seated in the front row and made a spectacular catch.[187] There was one out, and the bases remained loaded. The left-handed-hitting Isbell was the next batter. His plate appearance, with Pfiester in his windup, the three base runners taking huge leads and the Cubs infield and outfield both drawn in, was captured in the photograph on page 81. Pfiester struck Isbell out swinging at a curve ball for the second out. With two outs, Chance's infield was able to return to normal fielding depth. At the same time, Cubs fans were breathing sighs of relief, knowing Pfiester needed to retire the next batter, the light-hitting George Rohe, to escape the inning unscathed. They likely thought that Rohe could not possibly repeat his unlikely heroics of Game One. Lightning, however, would strike twice.

Allegedly, when Rohe took his place in the batter's box, Cubs catcher Johnny Kling began trash-talking, calling Rohe a "lucky stiff" for getting a high fastball in the first game, which Rohe had lashed for a triple. Kling further called Rohe a "Busher," telling him that there's no way he would see that same high fastball again.[188] Of course, that is exactly what Pfiester threw, but Rohe was not fooled. He slammed a long drive down the left-field line that took one hop into the outfield crowd for a ground-rule triple. All three runners scored, and the Sox rode Walsh the rest of the way to a two-hit shutout and a 3–0 victory in Game Three. For the second time in three days, the unheralded Rohe had become the unlikeliest of World Series heroes.

Newspaper stories after the game pointed out that had Hahn successfully bunted instead of being hit by a pitch in the nose, he would have become the first out of the inning. Given that Isbell and Jones were then both retired, Rohe never would have come to bat that inning, and the Sox would not have scored. The *Washington Post* punned that the White Sox "literally [won] by a nose."[189]

As American League president Ban Johnson left the park, he shouted, "It was one of the greatest battles I ever saw anywhere." He then boasted, "There is nothing more to it now but the shouting."[190] Patsy Donovan, manager of the Brooklyn Superbas, reflected the National League perspective: "I think Chance and his men may have underrated the ability of the Sox. Possibly they expected a sort of a walkover, and they are shocked and surprised at the defense they are running up against. Another thing is, that the Cubs have never been through a serious strain like a stretch of games of this kind....While the Nationals look stronger as a team, after all the big test is in the pitcher's box, and if they can't hit Walsh and Altrock, it's all over with them."[191]

////

South Side alderman "Fighting Charlie" Martin celebrated the White Sox victory that night, along with his friend Rod Laverty, with "liquid enthusiasm" at the bar of the Stratford Hotel.[192] With each passing hour, their "enthusiasm" heightened, until they proceeded to get into a shouting match with a "stranger" who did not take kindly to their "vociferous" boasting about the team. When told by the bartender to keep it down, the sloshed alderman boasted that he was "an alderman from the stockyards."[193] He and Laverty then proceeded to chase the stranger into the hotel lobby, which was packed with baseball fans. A brawl ensued, with Alderman Martin and Laverty striking the hotel's house detective several times. A patrol wagon was called, but Martin and Laverty were somehow able to make it out of the hotel before the wagon arrived.

Apparently oblivious, in their inebriated state, to the risk that returning to the scene of the crime might present, their apparent unquenchable thirst caused Martin and Laverty to return to the hotel bar. When the bartender refused to serve them, the two became belligerent once again, and they were ultimately grabbed by police. Showing his aldermanic badge, Martin threatened, "Don't you try to arrest me, I'm Alderman Martin."[194] Of course, his intoxicated utterances had little deterrent effect on the officers, who tossed him, along with Laverty, in a wagon for a ride to the Central Police Station. There, a battalion of police, aware of "Fighting Charlie"

Martin's pugilistic reputation, were on hand to greet him. He and Laverty were booked on charges of disorderly conduct and then put into a wagon that would take them to the Harrison Street Police Station for lockup. On the way there, the wagon made a stop at Hinky Dink Kenna's saloon, where they picked up the ward alderman. When the wagon arrived at Harrison Street Station, Kenna was happy to write a bail bond for his fellow "baseball enthusiasts" and city council member.

By this time, however, Alderman Martin was so exhausted and intoxicated that he was in no condition to walk on his own, so little Hinky Dink tossed Martin over his shoulder and somehow managed to drag him, staggering and weaving, to a taxi for a ride home.[195]

////

Despite the Cubs being down two games to one in the series, Cubs fans gathered in a strong show of support outside the Thirty-Ninth Street gates prior to Game Four, cheering as the team arrived in carriages shortly after 1:00 p.m. The players basked not only in the adoration of the fans but also in the warm, summer-like sunshine that had been missing for the first three games. Fans, having grown accustomed to bringing their fur and wearing warm winter coats, felt uncomfortably warm. The weather brought out the biggest crowd of the World Series to date, over eighteen thousand.

For the South Siders, the warm weather helped George Davis with his bad back, and he was ready to start his first game of the series, replacing Tannehill at short. On the other hand, Eddie Hahn arrived at the ballpark with his nose in a cast after being hit with a curveball the day before. On Hahn's arrival, Chance approached him and asked how he was doing, telling him that he had worried all night about the injury.[196] Like Davis, Hahn was ready to play.

On the mound, there was a repeat of Game One, with Mordecai Brown starting for the West Siders and Altrock for the South Siders. Both pitchers dominated the first six innings, aided by spectacular defensive plays turned in by both teams. For the White Sox, Hahn, who refused to be sidelined despite his broken nose, backed up against the steel wire that separated the outfield from the circus seats, leaped and snared a long drive by Kling over the heads of those in the crowd. Otherwise, it would have gone for a ground-rule triple. For the Cubs, Evers sparkled in the field, at least twice robbing Sox batters of what appeared to be sure hits.

84

At the top of the seventh, the game remained scoreless. Chance led off the inning with a single to right, well over the head of second baseman Isbell. Steinfeldt bunted Chance over to second. Two outs later, with Chance on third, Evers came to the plate. Evers ripped Altrock's first pitch over the head of George Rohe at third for a single, and Chance crossed the plate with the game's first and, ultimately, only run.

In the bottom of the ninth, with the Cubs leading, 1–0, Brown was quickly able to retire the first two batters. Manager Jones, however, was then able to work Brown for a walk. Then, when a passed ball deflected off the umpire's shoe, Jones wound up standing on second with the potential tying run. A hit could tie the game. Isbell, the next batter, scorched a liner up the middle that looked destined for center field to tie the game. But Brown stuck out his hand and blocked the liner. It knocked Brown completely off his feet. He recovered, retrieved the ball and threw to Chance to retire Isbell, ending the game.[197] Brown had held the Sox to just two hits over nine innings in recording a 1–0 World Series shutout.

The series now stood tied at two games apiece. Manager Jones was disappointed but not discouraged because of the loss. He said, "Well, it's even up now, and with Walsh to work tomorrow and again later, if necessary, I think that we have quite an advantage. The Cubs cannot hit the spitball and all we have to do is get a run or two. I am more confident than ever of winning the series."[198]

On the other hand, Chance was thrilled with the victory. "The Sox are putting up a great fight against us, and I can see nothing but victory ahead of us from now on. I do not believe that the series will go the full limit. By Sunday night I expect my boys to be the world's champions."[199] Chance was correct that the series would not go the full limit, but not in the way he expected.

////

The pivotal fifth game of the World Series returned to West Side Grounds, along with summerlike weather. A massive crowd gathered outside the gates, trying to get in. The largest crowd of the series, more than twenty-three thousand, would be shoehorned into the ballpark. Despite the beautiful weather, the comforts of playing at home and the throng of Cubs supporters, the 116-win Cubs curiously entered the contest without their usual swagger, instead taking action intended to inexplicably bring good luck. The Cubs were concerned that they had not yet won at home in the series, so Chance and the Cubs decided to wear their traveling gray uniforms for this home game. Additionally, to try to bring good luck, a pair of young bear cubs were led onto the field as mascots as part of pregame activities. The cubs were tethered by chains to their handlers from Lincoln Park Zoo. The cubs were then trotted around the bases.

By game time, every seat in the ballpark was filled. The gates were closed to those gathered outside more than an hour before the contest. Nonetheless, just before game time, additional seating was found. Consequently, a few lucky hundred were allowed into the ballpark just before the first pitch. The rooftops south of the ballpark on Taylor Street were packed. Fans desperate to see the game even climbed trees and poles. Many other fans who were unable to get into the park stood outside the gates, listening to the periodic roars and outbursts of the crowd inside, trying to decipher their significance and guessing just what had happened and by which team.

An anecdote associated with the game involved one of the fans in the crowd, a prominent West Side Irishman and ardent Cubs fan named "Fog" Finnegan. Prior to Game Five, Fog was seated with a group of fans surrounded by a mostly pro–White Sox crowd. Fog stood on his seat and taunted the Sox fans, daring them to place wagers with him. Shouting that the Cubs would prevail handily, Fog offered them odds accordingly. The Sox fans, however, refused to give him the time of day. Relentlessly, Fog continued his taunting. Then, when the lineups were announced, Fog was stunned to learn that the White Sox battery would consist of two fellow Irishmen, Walsh and Sullivan. Fog sat and balanced his allegiance to the Cubs and his fondness for his home country. Standing on his seat again, Fog changed his tune. Not only did he cease his taunting of Sox fans, but instead he loudly voiced a sudden fondness for his countrymen, Walsh and Sullivan, and abruptly changed his wager, now offering odds in line with an expected victory, not by his beloved West Side Cubs, but rather by his new favorites sporting Irish origins, the Sox![200]

Both starting pitchers, Reulbach and Walsh, had been superb in their earlier series starts. Each had allowed only two hits, Reulbach in Game Two and Walsh in Game Three. Most fans anticipated a low-scoring contest. But things did not go so well for either starter in Game Five.

The Sox drew first blood in the first inning, scoring one run. They would have conceivably scored more but for fine fielding by Johnny Evers. In the Cubs' half of the first, the Sox—who had fielded so well during the regular season—played giveaway. The Cubs put together two singles, a hit batsman and a fielder's choice to go along with a throwing error by second baseman

Isbell and another throwing error by Walsh to take a 3–1 lead after the first inning. After that, however, the game—and the World Series itself—tilted in favor of the South Side.

The previously slumping Isbell led off the South Siders' half of the third inning with his second double of the game, and Davis followed with a double of his own, scoring Isbell and making the score 3–2, Cubs. Manager Chance then decided he had seen enough of Reulbach and chose to go with Jack Pfiester in relief, who had started and pitched well in a 3–0 loss in Game Three. Pfiester was able to strike out Rohe for the first out. After a walk and a fielder's choice, the Sox had two outs and runners at first and third, down by a run. The White Sox pulled off a daring double steal, with Davis crossing the plate, tying the game, 3–3.

Leading off the top of the fourth, Sox pitcher Walsh coaxed a walk out of Pfiester. It was the third time in five games a Cubs pitcher had walked his counterpart. Things went downhill after that for Pfiester, and the Sox scored three runs in the inning. After that, Chance replaced Pfiester with Orval Overall. Like his predecessor, Overall walked the first batter he faced that inning, Rohe. When Donohue followed with a double to left—the third double of the inning—Davis scored with the Sox's fourth run of the inning. The Cubs added one run in their half of the fourth. White Sox 7, Cubs 4 after four innings.

In the sixth, the Sox scored once, and the Cubs tallied twice in their half of the inning, making the score 8–6. With two outs and nobody on in the Cubs' half of the eighth, Sheckard hit a ground ball that eluded Isbell. Incredibly, it was the sixth error by the White Sox in the game, and yet they still held a two-run lead. The Cubs could not score Sheckard that inning.

The Cubs threatened again but did not score in the ninth, and the Sox had their third victory of the series, 8–6. The previously slumping Isbell had four doubles and scored three runs in Game Five, and the Hitless Wonders of the regular season exploded for eight runs and twelve hits. The Chicago baseball world had been turned upside down, as the Hitless Wonders' offense exploded and the formidable Cubs' pitching staff imploded. The Sox were one victory from an improbable world championship.

That night, a Boston newspaper reporter in Chicago wrote: "Tonight, the city is nearly crazy over the series, and one hears no other subject discussed. Even the women folks of the South Side are wearing white hose in honor of their favorite team, while the elite of the West Side have purchased all of the little toy bears in town."[201]

////

Lost amid all the World Series frenzy of that evening, October 13, 1906, was a dinner gathering of the entire membership of the Merchants Club, all of whom had come to hear Daniel Burnham speak about his new plans to improve and beautify the city. The Merchants Club apparently liked what they heard. In little more than two weeks, the Merchants Club would hold its first formal meeting to develop what later became known as the "Plan of Chicago."

////

For Game Six, nearly twenty thousand fans jammed the White Sox home stadium at Thirty-Ninth and Wentworth, and thousands waited in the streets. A Boston writer said that he "never saw such a crowd. It was packed late into every corner of the grounds and two-thirds of those in it were rooting for the Sox. There were ten thousand frenzied fans standing around outside the fence and crowding the nearby streets, as well as the housetops in the vicinity, simply willing to remain and receive verbal reports from those on top of the fence."[202] Cops were posted to make sure that none of the fans would attempt to hop the fences.[203]

Now in a must-win situation, Chance was in a dilemma. Normally, in such a crucial game, he would go with his most stalwart starter, Mordecai Brown. But Brown had already pitched in Game One and had just thrown a complete-game shutout in Game Four. On top of that, he was coming off a sore arm that had bothered him at season's end. If Chance decided to go with Brown again, he would be asking the pitcher to do so with only one day of rest between starts. The *Washington Post* offered that "the bombardment of Reulbach and Pfiester yesterday had worried the Cub leader to the point where he was able to place no faith in any of his staff but Brown."[204] With nowhere else for Chance, in his own mind, to turn, he decided to gamble and go with Brown to start Game Six. It was a gamble that would not pay off.

To open Game Six of the 1906 World Series on the South Side, the Cubs scored one run in the top of the first inning off Sox starter Doc White. The White Sox, however, then pummeled Brown, scoring three in their half of the first and four more in the second, knocking Brown out of the game. In the first, Schulte attempted to track down Davis's fly ball to right field. The ball was headed to the crowd seated in the outfield. The crowd, in turn, was being monitored and held back by a policeman. Accounts differ as to what happened next.

Both Schulte and center fielder Hofman would both protest vehemently that the police officer—possibly an overzealous rooter of the Sox—had risen from his seat and jostled, or at least interfered with, Schulte's attempt to make the catch. The ball then landed safely. Schulte claimed that but for the interference he would have made the play. Charles Dryden, reporting for the *Tribune*, backed up Schulte's account, writing that the policeman kicked Schulte.[205]

On the other hand, Sox fans argued that Schulte had slowed up too early and simply made a poor play. Contrary to Dryden's account in the *Tribune*, the *Washington Post* corroborated Sox fans' accounts: "No direct interference was seen from the stand. It simply looked as if the right fielder played the ball badly."[206] With no instant replay available in those days, the umpire's call stood.

In any event, the play seemed to confirm Fullerton's pre-series prediction that the Cubs' superiority in outfield defense would be mitigated by the restrictions on available space brought on by the insertion of outfield seating. While Overall pitched well for the Cubs in relief of Brown, the huge early lead was insurmountable. According to the *Boston Globe*, "Capt. Chance saw that he was done for early in the game. The Cubs sat around the players' bench as nervous as old hens, while the Sox grinned and made matters worse by offering bluff consolation."[207] When Schulte grounded to pitcher Doc White to end the game, the Hitless Wonders had won for the second straight game and captured a world's championship. The final was 8–3. Sox fans stormed the field, and players from both teams rushed to escape the bedlam they knew was coming. When some of the players reached their carriages outside of the ballpark, the drivers were unable to get away because of the enthusiastic crowds surrounding them.[208]

Cubs' president Murphy was gracious in defeat: "The best team won. Too much praise cannot be given to Pres. Comiskey and Capt. Jones and the team which by unprecedented pluck climbed in midseason from seventh place to the top of their own league, and then topped off that great accomplishment by winning the world's championship from the team that made a runaway race of the National League contest. I call for three cheers for Comiskey and his great team."[209]

Frank Chance, on the other hand, couldn't hide his bitterness after the defeat. He said, "There is one thing I will never believe, and that is the Sox are better than the Cubs."[210]

Afterward, a huge throng of Sox fans embarked on a circuit to visit the homes of the White Sox players living on that part of the South Side. The first home to be visited was that of Game Six winner Doc White. But White was not at home, so the crowd headed for the home of manager Fielder Jones. Along the route, an alert fan spotted shortstop George Davis in a restaurant. Leaders of the crowd persuaded Davis to leave his table and join the crowd on the sidewalk. Davis graciously answered their questions and entertained them with his take on the series. They put Davis on their shoulders and carried him as they continued to the home of Jones.

As luck would have it, the crowd not only found Jones at home but also found that he happened to be entertaining Doc White at the time. Jones graciously thanked the crowd for their support. White then suggested that the crowd next pay a visit to George Rohe.[211] Leaving Davis's home, the fans stormed down Thirty-Sixth Street toward Rohe's residence, located in the Hotel Hayden. Residents from the otherwise quiet neighborhood joined the raucous mob, and all clamored for Rohe to make an appearance. He finally appeared in the window of his second-story apartment, tossing out a stuffed, six-foot-long white stocking, to the delight of the crowd.[212]

Sox fans also relished Cubs fans settling up their bets. On Milwaukee Avenue, two humiliated Cubs fans harnessed to a carriage pulled two laughing Sox fans.[213] Later in December, other Cubs fans would pay up on their bets by taking the plunge into frozen Lake Michigan.[214]

Elsewhere on the South Side, bonfires lit up the night. In fact, a huge bonfire on the 8300 block of South Cottage Grove Avenue had to be extinguished by firemen.[215] The party lasted until around dawn.[216] Cubs fans, on the other hand, "stayed home and mourned."[217]

At the end of the World Series, Comiskey handed Fielder Jones a check for $15,000, or $1,874 per White Sox player. The players were initially appreciative of Comiskey's apparent generosity. But they later realized that the check was meant not as a bonus but as a significant down payment on their 1907 salaries. The players were outraged, team cohesion disintegrated and 1907 became a lost season for the 1906 champions.[218]

Chapter 4

FALL 1906

The Postseason City Tournament

T he 1906 World Series did not end baseball in Chicago for that year, and it did not even end baseball for the Cubs and White Sox. The contracts of the major leaguers for the season had just expired, and the players took the position that there were no legal restrictions preventing them from further supplementing their World Series checks by playing postseason exhibitions against highly regarded and widely followed semipro teams.

As historian Ray Schmidt has pointed out, in the early 1900s, Major League Baseball was not the only popular form of baseball entertainment in town. Semipro baseball had a huge fan base. The semipro teams played in various city leagues, most of which were sponsored by corporations, civic organizations and even churches.[219] Semipro players were usually paid but generally did not rely on their baseball income to live on. Instead, most semipro players had regular jobs and primarily played for the love of the game on weekends.

There were numerous enclosed ballparks throughout the city to accommodate semipro baseball, and in the years after 1900, fan attendance at the weekend games continued to grow. Sizable crowds on occasion numbered as many as four thousand for a single semipro game. Fan interest in semipro baseball was high, and newspapers gave substantial coverage to semipro games as well as major league games. As a result, early 1900s Chicago baseball fans were not unlike modern-day sports fans who follow football, basketball and other sports at both the professional and collegiate levels.

Left: Semi-pro Gunthers captain Nick Pedroes. *Chicago History Museum.*

Opposite: White Sox player Jiggs Donahue. *Chicago History Museum.*

By 1906, Chicago's best semipro teams were the Gunthers, the West Ends and the Logan Squares.[220] The Gunthers were organized by prominent Chicago businessman Charles Gunther and played their home games at a ballpark at Clark and Leland on the North Side.[221] The West Ends, as their name implies, were based on the West Side at Madison and Cicero.[222] The Logan Squares were founded by possibly the best-known semipro player of the early 1900s, former major league pitcher Jimmy Callahan, He twice had twenty-win seasons for the Cubs and had also pitched for the White Sox before forming the semipro Logan Squares.[223]

By 1906, Callahan had assembled a group of talented semipro players and several former major league players, including former Cubs pitcher Long Tom Hughes, and even some current major leaguers. His Logan Squares were a formidable team and were considered by some to be "professional," with salaried players.[224] Callahan even had the funding to build a new stadium, Logan Square Park, on the Northwest Side at Diversey and Milwaukee.[225]

With the 1906 World Series over and semipro baseball enjoying unprecedented popularity, both the Cubs and Sox players saw, and jumped

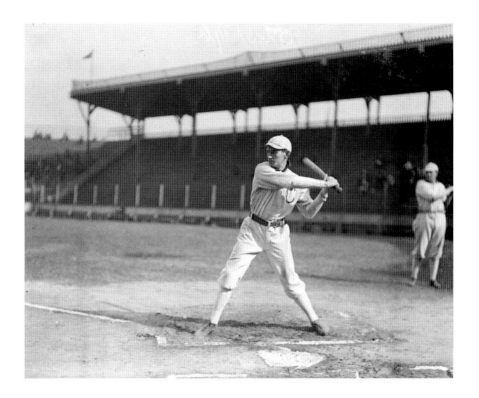

at, the opportunity to earn some extra postseason cash. On the weekend of October 20 and 21, 1906, the NL champion Cubs and the world champion White Sox each played two semipro teams, the Logan Squares and Gunthers, in an exhibition elimination city tournament.[226] The semipro parks where the tournament series was played were jammed with fans.[227]

In the tournament, the Cubs used many of the same regulars who had played in the World Series. Evers, on the other hand, was not present, as he returned home to Troy, New York, to receive a joyous hometown welcome and parade. Neither Steinfeldt nor Kling participated in the exhibitions, either. But Chance, Tinker, Schulte, Brown and Hofman played. The Sox exhibition team was managed by Jiggs Donohue. Rohe, Hahn, Sullivan and Altrock were among seven regulars in the lineup.[228]

The semipro Gunthers lost both of their games to the Cubs on Saturday and the Sox on Sunday. The Logan Squares fared much better. On Saturday, they beat the world champion White Sox, 2–1, with Jimmy Callahan besting his former team and Sox twenty-game winner Nick Altrock.[229] This left the two Saturday winners, the Cubs and the Logan Squares, to face each other Sunday for the championship of the exhibition tournament at Logan Square

Park. In the series finale, the Cubs pitched their ace, Three Finger Brown, who that day gave up only four hits to the Logan Squares, two of which were to Callahan. But the Cubs could not solve the opponent's pitcher, Hughes. The Logan Squares pushed a run across in the tenth to pull off a stunning 1–0, ten-inning victory.[230]

After the game, delirious supporters in the crowd carried the Logan Squares players around the stadium in a wild celebration.[231] With Hughes, who had just thrown a ten-inning shutout, the fans were especially raucous and rough. He "lost parts of his uniform before the police could rescue him from the joyful rooters."[232] Amazingly, in winning the city tournament, the 1906 semipro Logan Squares had beaten both the world champion White Sox and the National League champion Cubs on consecutive days![233]

////

Over the course of the summer, representatives of the Merchants Club of Chicago and the Commercial Club had begun informal discussions with Daniel Burnham concerning the possibility of putting together a plan for Chicago. By the time the World Series was over, it was time for discussions to be taken to a higher level. On October 29, 1906, just two weeks after the conclusion of the only all-Chicago World Series, the first official meeting of members of the Merchants Club was held to discuss a comprehensive plan that would alleviate traffic congestion, promote business, beautify the city and improve the physical and mental health of its citizens. Three years later, the finalized plan became known as the "Plan of Chicago," or the "Burnham Plan." That meeting was the first of several hundred held over the course of the next three years. While Burnham was not present at that first meeting, he was present and took charge at many others.

At a meeting on December 13, 1906, the plan committee decided on its first course of action: prioritizing and focusing on a "boulevard-link" connecting the North and South Sides at the Chicago River.[234] The bridges then crossing the river were woefully inadequate to accommodate both commercial and noncommercial traffic, leading to extensive congestion. To remedy the situation, the committee planned a two-deck bridge over Michigan Avenue, with commercial traffic relegated to the lower deck and other traffic free to use the upper deck.

At another of those later meetings, Burnham advised the group that he would provide his services free of charge and limit the expenses incurred on the project, which he estimated to be $25,000, a huge sum in those days. Later, when the costs eventually ran approximately $10,000 over budget, Burnham reached into his own pockets to cover the overage.[235] In his willingness to advance—at considerable personal sacrifice, time and effort—the cause of civic improvement while foregoing any pecuniary benefit for himself, Burnham proved to be the antithesis of Coughlin and Kenna.

PART IV
1907

Chapter 1

POISED FOR REDEMPTION

The 1907 Cubs started the season knowing that they had unfinished business. The previous year's World Series had left a bad taste in their mouths all winter, and the Cubs were ready to make amends. The roster of the 1906 pennant-winning team was intact, and the Cubs started the season on fire. But so did the hated Giants.

By May 20, the Cubs were 23-4, while the Giants were one game better at 24-3. Covering the end of 1906 and the beginning of 1907, the Cubs had a streak in which they won 122 of 154 contests.[236] With both teams on hot streaks, an early season showdown series at the Polo Grounds beckoned for the National League's two powerhouse teams. On May 21, 1907, the Cubs faced the Giants for the first time that season, with New York leading Chicago by a game. A bitter rivalry was developing between the NL entries representing the two largest cities in America, and civic pride was on the line whenever these two teams met.

The Cubs-Giants rivalry was intensified by the personalities of their respective tough-as-nails managers, Frank Chance and John McGraw. McGraw was one of the Cubs' great antagonists during the first decade of the twentieth century and another of baseball's more colorful characters. He learned how the game was played early in his career as a player in Baltimore, when he and his teammates "bullied umpires, tricked the opposing teams, tampered with equipment, [and] doctored the diamond."[237] Later, as a manager, one of McGraw's players, Fred Snodgrass, said that "[h]e had the most vicious tongue of any man who ever lived."[238]

While small in stature, McGraw was "as rough as the next fellow and twice as ready to fight."[239] In Cincinnati, he offered to fight everyone in the park, leading Giants outfielder Mike Donlin to say, "He's a wonder. He can start more fights, and win fewer, than anyone I ever saw."[240]

McGraw's propensity for pugilism once, however, led to a humorous ending. Ned Swartwood, a "big, good" National League umpire, once ran the diminutive McGraw out of a game, and the manager was furious. After the game, McGraw tracked down Swartwood under the stands near the spot where a bridge just outside traversed a small creek. "I've got a notion to take a punch at your jaw," snarled McGraw. The much larger Swartwood good-naturedly stuck out his jaw. To his astonishment, McGraw actually punched him. Swartwood then picked up the little man and threw him into the creek. In doing so, Swartwood's momentum caused him to fall off the bridge and into the creek as well. The two men crawled out on opposite banks, "their tempers cooled, and sat, dripping and muddy, laughing at each other."[241]

With his aggressive, antagonistic tendencies, McGraw naturally seemed to encounter hostility wherever he went. Nonetheless, he did not hesitate to invite even more hostility by making up fake stories designed to rile up opposing fans, if that was what it took to draw attention and fans to the ballpark. For instance, manufacturing or embellishing any perceived threat against him, McGraw would wire ahead to the chief of police in the next city the Giants were visiting, asking for protection from its citizens. Newspapers in that city would publish the text of the wire, and fans would turn out, livid, to the ballpark.

But John McGraw was much more than an instigator itching for a fight. His personality was multifaceted, and with few exceptions, his players loved playing for him. Giants outfielder Al Bridwell said: "He was a fighter, but he was also the kindest, best-hearted fellow you ever saw.…He knew how to handle men.…He got the most out of each man."[242] McGraw would lay down the law, and he would not tolerate a player lying to him, nor would he tolerate mental errors or errors in judgment. McGraw would rip a player— or worse—for committing such an error. One time, he fined a player who had just hit a home run because he had missed a bunt sign. But after ripping or disciplining a player, McGraw never brought it up again. The transgression was forgotten; no grudge was held.

In contrast with mental errors, however, McGraw treated fielding errors or failures to get a hit as part of the game, and when his players took heat from the press or other critics for such regular errors or hitting failures,

New York Giants manager John McGraw. *Chicago History Museum.*

he would "fight for his players and protect them."[243] In fact, when Giants outfielder Fred Snodgrass was unfairly blamed for costing the Giants the 1912 World Series after dropping a routine fly ball, McGraw not only took no action against Snodgrass, he also gave him a $1,000 raise.[244] New York pitcher Rube Marquard summed up what most Giants thought of McGraw: "What a great man he was!"[245]

Just as McGraw was willing to fight for his players, his players were willing to fight for him, and the Giants adopted McGraw's combativeness against their opponents. And McGraw's combativeness inspired the same in Giants fans. Already once in the 1907 season Giants fans had rioted after a game. Now, on May 21, it was about to happen again.

////

Anticipation was high before the May 21 matchup between the two rivals and league leaders, the Cubs and Giants. A crowd of twenty-two thousand filled the Polo Grounds. Throughout the game, the partisan crowd felt that, time after time, their boys were getting the short end of the stick from the two-man umpiring crew of Hank O'Day and Bob Emslie, and they frequently voiced their displeasure. According to the *New York Times*, by the ninth inning, when a Giants defeat seemed imminent, "the unsportsmanlike spectators had worked themselves into a wholly unreasonable temper." On the last play of the game, when New York base runner Roger Bresnahan was called out by Emslie on a tag play, Bresnahan complained bitterly—even though his errors in the field were the prime cause for the Giants' loss.[246]

Incited by Bresnahan's outburst, which only furthered their anger over their team's loss, the fans were no longer content with expressing their displeasure from the stands. Nearly half of the crowd stormed the field, heaping verbal abuse on players but reserving their most caustic words for the umpires. Then a "missile" was tossed at Emslie. After that, the crowd began tossing lemons, cushions and anything else they could get their hands on. The Pinkerton private security force labored to make their way to the center of the melee. Unable to easily make their way through the thick and enraged crowd, the Pinkertons drew their revolvers and threatened to open fire. This made an impression on some of those standing near the local police, clearing some room, but it did nothing to clear a path for them beyond that. Fearing that the situation would escalate, one of the Pinkertons fired a shot in the air to summon help from the police force stationed outside the stadium.[247]

Not only did this shot summon help, but it also had a sobering effect on many in the rampaging crowd, who were coming to realize the true gravity of the situation. The officers who rushed into the stadium were thus able to make it to the point where the real roughnecks were causing trouble. They cordoned off a path, allowing the umpires to finally reach the clubhouse. After all of this, fortunately, no one in the melee—police, players or umpires—was seriously hurt.[248]

////

Raising of the 1906 National League pennant at West Side Grounds. *Library of Congress.*

The Cubs and Giants—still the two top teams in the standings—would meet again in early June in another three-game showdown series, this time at West Side Grounds. By now, the Cubs were in first place, having taken over on May 28. Chicago took the first two games in the series. For the third and final game of the series, twenty-five thousand spectators, possibly the largest regular-season crowd in the history of West Side Grounds to that point, turned out.[249] In that game, Three Finger Brown masterfully dispatched the Giants, 4–3, in two hours and five minutes. Johnny Kling hit two doubles and scored one run, and his ninth-inning bunt was critical in scoring the game-winning run.

The victory gave the Cubs a sweep of the series. It elevated the Cubs' record to 35-9 and swelled their lead over second-place New York to five and a half games. They would never relinquish that lead.

By July 4, the Cubs already held an eleven-and-a-half-game lead. Chicago's success at that point of the season enhanced the celebratory mood when they raised the 1906 pennant over West Side Grounds in a festive Independence Day ceremony that morning. The team's supporters were thrilled by the celebration, which included cannon fire and explosions. They were even more thrilled when the team took both games of a doubleheader from Cincinnati later that afternoon.[250]

// // //

A few days later, on July 9, the Cubs boasted a league-leading record of 54-17 and visited Brooklyn to play the Superbas. With the Cubs leading 5–0 late in the game, some fans in the cheap seats apparently took exception to the fact that the home team was losing. Several soda bottles suddenly flew out of the stands and rolled their way to the feet of first baseman Frank Chance. He picked up one of the bottles and glared back at the bottle throwers. More bottles then flew from the stands toward Chance, who then lost his temper. With a bottle already in his hand, he heaved it into the crowd. That triggered an even greater barrage of bottles from the crowd, during which Chance stood in defiance, like "Mr. Ajax," before his harassers. He picked up a second bottle and heaved it into the crowd.[251]

The crowd was now incensed and out for Chance's blood. They would have likely tried to kill Chance but were restrained by a formidable screen separating the crowd from the field. Fortunately, Brooklyn president Charles Ebbets intervened and appeased the crowd by telling them that he would have Chance arrested. Chance then received a police escort to the clubhouse, where he sat with detectives waiting for the fans' tempers to cool. Some of the "blood seekers," however, lingered outside the ballpark's front entrance for over an hour, hoping for the opportunity to retaliate against Chance.[252]

By that time, the detectives sitting with Chance thought it safe for him to make a run for it to the elevated train station a block away. Ebbets, however, not wanting to risk any further trouble, arranged for Chance to join him and three cops in an armored car to allow Chance to escape back to his New York hotel.[253]

After the incident, Chance was remorseful and apologetic. He realized he had made the biggest mistake of his career. His two throws had hit a man and a boy; fortunately, nobody was seriously hurt. Nonetheless, he would be suspended by the National League and told by the police not to return to Brooklyn for the rest of the series.[254]

////

In August, the Cubs and Giants renewed their heated rivalry in New York. When Frank Chance arrived at the Polo Grounds, he found waiting for him a letter purportedly from the murderous gang known as the Black Hand. The letter, in legible handwriting and proper spelling indicative of someone literate and well-versed in English, contained "disjointed English" that appeared to create the impression that "the writer was an illiterate foreigner."[255] The letter read as follows:

> *Manager Chance, Chicago National League of the Baseball Club—*
> *Dear Sir: Your club must not get again Pennant this year 1907 from the*
> *New York, and you will let New York club will have Pennant championship*
> *of the year 1907 from your club. Your club are too coward, but "Poor*
> *Giants."*
> *If you do not let the Giants from the first place this year, Gang of Black*
> *Hands will see you after, will help you for your life. Look out for danger life.*
> *We will use bomb on your players team on train wreck and we will follow*
> *your team travelling.*
> *No fear to tell Policeman, but my powerful than them.*
> *New York must have Pennant this year from your club.*
> *We are cranky on Giants.*
> *Yours truly*   *BLACK HANDS* [256]

As one might expect, Chance not only dismissed the crank letter, he also played that day in a big Cubs win. The life-threatening consequences that the letter portended never occurred, and the only life that was jeopardized, after that day's Cubs victory, was the little life the Giants had left in the pennant race.

The Cubs clinched the pennant with plenty of time to spare on September 23, when they defeated the Phillies, 4–1, in a rain-shortened game. Incredibly, that victory included not only a steal of home by Evers but also a triple play pulled off by the Chicago infield.[257]

While the 1907 Cubs did not achieve the 116 victories of the previous season, their final record of 107-46 was good enough to capture the NL pennant by 17 games over eventual second-place Pittsburgh, who were led by future Hall of Famer Honus Wagner.

The Cubs winning the pennant in such dominant fashion was even more impressive because their Peerless Leader, Frank Chance, missed one-third of the season with injuries, and Tinker, Schulte and Kling missed significant time as well. Furthermore, the 1907 Cubs hitters did not perform as well as they had the previous season, but defense and pitching compensated for any offensive letdown.

Throughout the season, Kling excelled with his defensive skills and handling of pitchers. In recent years, before the 2023 rule change enlarging the bases, the average catcher threw out less than 30 percent of base runners attempting to steal. Since the rule change, that percentage is even lower. But on June 21, 1907, Kling incredibly threw out all four Cardinal runners trying to steal in a 2–0 Chicago win.[258]

Even more remarkable was the Cubs' fabulous starting rotation of Brown, Pfiester, Overall and Reulbach. Orville Overall, the big Californian, emerged as the staff's top hurler with a 23-6 record. The staff's combined ERA for the season was an unimaginable 1.73, the best in baseball history. In fact, Brown, Pfiester, Overall and Reulbach are the top four pitchers on the post-1900 Cubs all-time best ERA list.

###

While the Cubs breezed to the 1907 National League pennant, the American League race between the Detroit Tigers and the Philadelphia A's was very tight. The Tigers featured star left fielder "Wahoo Sam" Crawford (a native of Wahoo, Nebraska), one of the great "sluggers" of the Deadball Era, and a young phenom named Ty Cobb. Cobb had always shown that he could play, but he was also brooding, violent and difficult to get along with in general. He got into brawls with his teammates and quickly earned an infamous reputation as a fighter. In an era when fighting was a common occurrence, Cobb stood out.[259] Tigers manager Hugh Jennings, on the other hand, was the antithesis of Cobb. Jennings was likeable, upbeat, outgoing and cheerful. He was also intelligent and well educated and had become a respected trial lawyer who practiced law in the offseason.[260] Jennings originally thought that Cobb was a liability to the Tigers and wanted to get rid of him. But he knew that Cobb had a passion to win, so Jennings cut him some slack both at the plate and on the basepaths.[261]

Cobb responded in 1907 by leading the AL in batting with a .350 average. Led by Cobb and Crawford, who batted .323,[262] the Tigers overtook the Philadelphia A's in late September for first place in the American League, and the Tigers never relinquished the lead.

On the evening of October 6, after Detroit clinched the pennant, celebrating Tigers fans became riotous. Some took over vacant properties in North Detroit and held them all day until police arrived. When the police arrived, the rioters greeted them with a shower of bricks and tried to tear down the structures on the occupied properties. Blazes lit up the night sky, and several arrests were made.[263]

In Chicago, there was a different reaction. When the Tigers clinched the pennant, a melancholy feeling passed over Cubs fans with the realization that the White Sox were out of the pennant race and there would be no repeat of the intensity of the 1906 "civil war" World Series. Nonetheless,

Tigers outfielder Ty Cobb. *Library of Congress.*

in a statement that would be incomprehensible to twenty-first-century Chicagoans, the *Tribune* predicted that all in the city, including Sox fans, were "sworn to allegiance" to the Cubs in their quest to keep the world championship in Chicago.[264]

Just imagine today's White Sox fans swearing allegiance to the Cubs!

Chapter 2

THE WORLD SERIES

The Cubs went into the 1907 World Series intent on finishing what they had set out to do at the beginning of the year: to earn redemption and capture their first World Series championship.

Game One, played at West Side Grounds, found the Cubs going with twenty-three-game winner Orval Overall. With the ballpark expanded with additional bleachers, a crowd of 24,377 was shoehorned inside. Game One would not be one of the finest for Detroit catcher Charlie Schmidt. To begin with, the Cubs were able to steal seven bases off Schmidt. Still, the Tigers held a 3–1 lead going into the ninth. Tiger fans, confident that victory would be theirs, made premature dashes for the exits. The Cubs, however, added a run in the ninth, making the score 3–2, and still had runners on second and third with two outs. Tigers pitcher "Wild Bill" Donovan then struck out pinch-hitter Del Howard, apparently giving Detroit a morale-boosting Game One victory. But the third strike rolled away from Schmidt. Instead of the Tigers recording the game's final out, Steinfeldt raced home from third, and the Cubs scored the tying run.[265]

Schmidt's dropped third strike is not nearly as prominent in baseball lore as Mickey Owens's famous dropped third strike in the 1941 World Series at Brooklyn's Ebbets Field. Owens's drop in the ninth inning opened the floodgates for the Yankees to rally after they appeared to have been beaten. Schmidt's dropped third strike with two outs in the ninth had a similar effect. It cost the Tigers their best shot at a World Series victory in 1907. Following the error, Game One went to twelve innings, after which darkness set in. With night baseball still a few years in the future, the game could not proceed and was adjudged a tie.[266] It would be the only game in the series in which the Tigers scored as many as three runs.

////

Schmidt would not be behind the plate for Detroit in Game Two at West Side Grounds. His replacement, Fred Payne, did not have much better luck than Schmidt had. The Cubs swiped five more bases in this game, and Pfiester limited Detroit to only one run in a 3–1 victory, allowing the Cubs to draw first blood in the series.

////

In Game Three, again played at West Side Grounds, Reulbach limited the Tigers to one run and just six hits. In the meantime, Evers's three hits led a Cubs attack that pummeled Detroit starter Ed Siever early and drove him from the game in the fourth. The Cubs cruised to a 5–1 victory. The World Series would now relocate to Detroit's Bennett Park for the next game, with the Cubs holding a two-games-to-none lead.

////

Prior to Game Four, fan frenzy seized Detroit, as the Tigers were about to host their first World Series game. Streets and hotels were jammed, and factories and stores were shut down to enable employees to partake in the excitement. From the onset of the game, the Tigers were physically and furiously going after Chance. With Chance at the plate in the first, pitcher Donovan hit him with a pitch on the hand, causing Chance to have his hand treated before he could resume play. Later, Ty Cobb slid into first base with spikes high, as if he had no concern about cutting the leg of Chance. The Peerless Leader took exception to that, and he and Cobb—two of the most notorious brawlers in the game—got into a heated verbal battle. No punches were thrown, however, and there was no physical alteration.[267]

In the third inning, with no score, Donovan, a good hitting pitcher, came to the plate. But the Cubs were ready. Donovan lashed a shot in the hole

The crowd at the October 12, 1907 World Series game in Detroit. *Library of Congress.*

between first and second into right field, but Schulte picked it up on a long bounce and immediately fired a strike to Chance at first, beating the embarrassed Donovan to the base and depriving the Tiger pitcher of a hit. That wasn't the only big defensive play turned in that day. Throughout the game, the Tigers hit Cubs starter Overall aggressively, but hard-hit line drive after line drive met "death in the malled paws of the Cubs."[268]

In the fourth inning, the Tigers took a 1–0 lead, but after a rain delay halted action in the fifth, the Cubs came roaring back. They scored two runs in the fifth, Overall driving in both with a single, and they iced the game by scoring three more in the seventh without hitting the ball out of the infield. In the meantime, Overall "baffled" Detroit hitters,[269] and the Cubs were one win from their first World Series championship with a 6–1 victory.

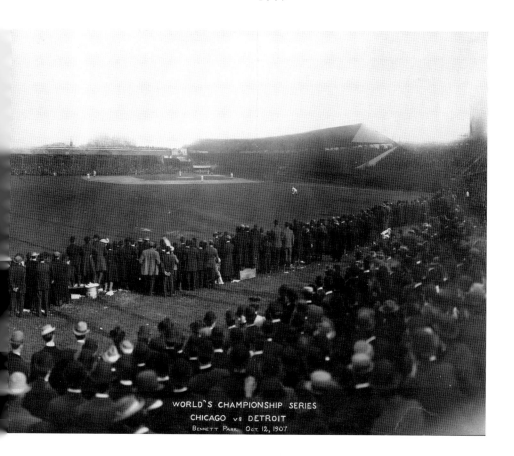

WORLD'S CHAMPIONSHIP SERIES
CHICAGO vs DETROIT
BENNETT PARK. OCT. 12, 1907

////

Game Five was played again in Detroit. With the Cubs up three wins to none with one tie, the Tigers were down to their last gasp, knowing that they needed to win four straight. A biting wind exacerbated already cold temperatures in the forties. Understandably, the crowd, which was expected to be eighteen thousand, did not even reach eight thousand. Many of the fans who did attend had made the trip from Chicago, hoping to witness firsthand the Cubs' first World Series championship.

Back in Chicago that same afternoon, for two hours, more than eight thousand fans packed Dearborn Street, from Madison to Monroe, to watch the *Tribune*'s electronic "scoreboard" re-create the events transpiring in Detroit. The massive crowds on Dearborn blanketed the entire width of the street as well as the sidewalks on both sides and exceeded the size of the crowd in attendance at the actual game in Detroit. So thick were the crowds on the street that traffic was halted, and attempts were made by police to create a path for those who, for some unknown reason, were attempting to get through the crowds for purposes of conducting business instead of intently following the scoreboards. In addition, for those unable to tolerate the outside cold, scoreboards were set up inside, as for the 1906 World Series, at the Auditorium and the Armory.[270] As the game started, the fans on Dearborn Street were exhilarated. The Cubs were one win away from their first world championship!

Chance sent Brown to the mound for Game Five. It was Brown's first start of the 1907 World Series. Unlike the final game of the 1906 World Series against the White Sox, Brown was well-rested, and he pitched brilliantly. The Cubs were able to score once in each of the first two innings, one run coming with the aid of a double steal. With each Cub run, the crowd on Dearborn Street boisterously yelled their approval. Brown would make those two runs stand up.

The Tigers mounted their biggest threat in the sixth, when Cobb doubled, but when he tried to steal third, Kling threw him out. Brown threw a shutout, and the final score was 2–0. It was the Cubs' fourth straight win in the series, following the tied first game. After the final out, Cubs fans swarmed the field in Detroit to offer congratulations to their heroes.[271] Frank Chance's boys had earned redemption. They were world champions!

⁂

The Cubs' victory celebration did not end in Detroit. A faster-than-expected train ride back to Chicago that night on the Michigan Central Railroad meant that the team was awakened the next morning having been shorted one hour of anticipated sleep. Groggy or not, the players were in good spirits when they later arrived at West Side Grounds to receive their due from their admiring supporters. No official time had been scheduled for the festivities to begin, and joyous throngs arrived hours before anything got underway. When proceedings finally got going, bands played, and the crowd sang. Chance, meanwhile, shook hands with hundreds of supporters. Then each of the Cubs was introduced, and each took his turn in addressing the crowd.

The world champions then treated the fans in the crowd to an exhibition split-squad game. When the Peerless Leader took his place behind the pitcher to call balls and strikes, the crowd was delighted. Chance took good-natured grief from players and fans throughout the game. As might be expected, the meaningless game turned into somewhat of a farce, as players played out of position, position players tried their hand at pitching and none of the players exhibited the hustle or intensity they had shown in beating the Tigers. Nonetheless, interest in whatever the new world champions were doing was so intense throughout the city that the *Tribune* saw fit to print the box score of the light-hearted exhibition in the next day's paper.[272]

Chapter 3

TWO CHICAGO CELEBRATIONS— ONE REFINED, ONE WRETCHED

On December 11, 1907, the magnates of baseball gathered in New York. Meetings were held during the day, and in the evening, Cubs president Charles Murphy hosted a classy banquet at the Waldorf-Astoria Hotel. The banquet celebrated the team's domination of the Tigers in the World Series. Over one hundred guests enjoyed a beautifully decorated venue in which top-quality cuisine was served and fine wine flowed.[273] President Murphy was a designated speaker and was treated to a song done in his honor.[274] For Murphy, it was a heady evening of personal pride and gratification. The admiration he would receive that evening, however, would contrast markedly with the repudiation a post–World Series banquet would bring him a year later.

////

Two days prior to the Cubs' elegant celebration at the Waldorf, Coughlin and Kenna had hosted a celebration of their own.[275] Their huge political gala, called the First Ward Ball, was an annual event held at the Coliseum in Chicago's First Ward. In stark contrast to the elegance and class of the Cubs' celebration at the Waldorf, the 1907 First Ward Ball featured appearances by the most notorious of Chicago's lowlifes, criminals and underworld figures engaged in drunken, tawdry and vulgar activities.

Wild parties were nothing new to Coughlin and Kenna. Starting in 1896, the two men had found a new and entertaining way to put the squeeze on their underworld constituents.[276] The First Ward Ball was held every year in December at the Coliseum at Fifteenth and Wabash. The ball was a means for Bathhouse John and Hinky Dink to extort cash from those of the underworld to whom the aldermanic duo offered, in a sense, "protection." As mandated by Coughlin, every prostitute, pimp, pickpocket, safecracker, bartender, gambler and thief had to buy at least one ticket, and brothel and saloon owners were required to buy many tickets. Consequences for noncompliance were severe. These illicit businesses could expect to be overrun by city inspectors, or worse, have their businesses shut down completely. Inside the event, madams had private boxes and sat side-by-side with city officials and politicians. The proceeds from the event went straight to the pockets of Coughlin and Kenna.

To bypass the city's midnight closing deadline for sales of alcohol, the ball was classified not as a political fundraiser but rather as a "charity" event, in which "education" was supposedly promoted. However, when asked to describe the educational benefits promoted by the ball, Kenna said, "It consists of hiring good halls and good speakers to teach the people of the First Ward to vote the straight Democratic ticket."[277]

The annual First Ward Ball had always been notorious for outrageous costumes, wild behavior, graft and decadence. Oftentimes, people who drank past their limit would pass out. Drunks would grope and sometimes tear off the clothing of unattended women. Men and women would sneak off to hook up.

The 1907 First Ward Ball was the wildest and most decadent party the city had seen up to that time. Nearly twenty thousand mostly disreputable people filled the Coliseum to overcapacity. The pickpockets, prostitutes, pimps, gamblers and swindlers were seen "marching arm in arm."[278] Many young people in attendance were simply drawn to the excitement. Guests drank immense quantities of beer and champagne and consumed a wagon-full of cigars. In the box seats, which were occupied by women wearing expensive clothing and jewelry, champagne was the drink of choice. Friendly contests took place among the ladies at the various tables. The objective was apparently to be the first to load their table with empty champagne bottles. The intensity of the contests seemed to increase as the piles of empty bottles began to reach the edges of the tables.[279]

Thousands of ladies also crowded the dance floor, but very few of the dancers wore the long gowns customary in that era for social occasions.

Shorter dresses were the order of the day, not necessarily for purposes of immodesty, but rather because the dancers avoided wearing "anything that could collect the germs from the floor."[280] Sexual advances made by drunks were rarely spurned. Critics of the ball decried the fact that "the shameful orgies of the so-called ball lasted throughout the night and scenes unmentionable among self-respecting men are said to have been undisputed and frequent." Those critics would add that "the debauch, which reminds one of pagan Rome in her most degenerate days, has been a prelude to the immoralities which are rife in the city today."[281]

The two promoters of the ball, however, had a different perspective: "This is the greatest ever," Coughlin bellowed. "I am delighted with the social success achieved by the First Ward Democratic club this evening. The hall seats 14,000, and you can see they are standing up in rows back of the seats in the gallery." Bathhouse's words were echoed by Hinky Dink Kenna: "It is far ahead of anything I saw in Paris during my recent European tour. There is nothing like it in the world. Could any other social function in Chicago attract a crowd like this? Not on your life. What are you having?"[282]

There may not have been anything like it in the rest of the world, but in the following year, 1908, Coughlin and Kenna would outdo themselves. The 1908 First Ward Ball would set even lower lows for depravity.

PART V
1908

Chapter 1

PRELUDE TO BASEBALL BEDLAM

The 1908 Cubs returned all the starting position players as well as all the mainstay pitchers from the 1907 world championship team. They started the season well and held a two-game lead on June 2. That same day, however, the Cubs sustained injuries to two players. Jimmy Sheckard and young infielder Heinie Zimmerman both ended up in the hospital. Sheckard's injury was especially serious, and his baseball career was nearly ended by a tragic accident. What happened, however, was something that the Cubs first tried to keep secret.

The Cubs' initial story was false. According to the team, Sheckard had turned his ankle while sliding into third base, and when he returned to the clubhouse to tend to his injury, Zimmerman suggested that Sheckard apply some ammonia to it. However, when Sheckard tried to remove the cap from the bottle, the bottle exploded, blinding Sheckard. Fortunately, he was rushed to a hospital right across the street, where his eye was satisfactorily treated.[283]

Later, however, the truth came out. In the locker room after the game, Sheckard said something to, or threw something at, the young infielder. Livid, Zimmerman picked up a bottle of ammonia and hurled it at Sheckard. The bottle broke as it hit Sheckard in the forehead between the eyes, spilling ammonia all over his face. The ammonia dripped into Sheckard's eyes, requiring the emergency trip to the hospital. Sheckard nearly lost the use of his left eye. While the hospital was able to save Sheckard's eyesight, he would miss thirty-nine games of the 1908 season.[284]

In the meantime, back in the locker room, manager Frank Chance immediately ran to Sheckard's assistance and confronted the younger Zimmerman. When it appeared that Zimmerman might be getting the better of Chance, the rest of the team joined their Peerless Leader, and Zimmerman was beaten to a pulp, requiring him to join Sheckard in the hospital. He missed numerous games.[285]

By August 16, injuries had taken their toll on Chicago. The Giants and Pirates had caught and passed the Cubs, and Chicago had fallen a full six games behind the league leaders. The challenge to overcome such a large deficit appeared daunting. Nonetheless, the Cubs won four of the next five and sliced the lead to three and a half games. Then they got hot. They embarked on a nine-game winning streak and caught the Giants. By the end of August, the Cubs and Giants were tied for first, and the Pirates trailed by only a half game.

The contest on September 4, 1908, in Pittsburgh drew little immediate attention, but it would have an enormous impact on the pennant race later. That day, the Pirates and Cubs were locked in a scoreless pitchers' duel into the bottom of the ninth. With two outs, a Pirate base hit scored the winning run. While this was occurring, the Pirate runner who was on first left the basepath and joined in the celebration with his teammates of a 1–0 victory. But he hadn't touched second base, which would have removed any chance for an inning-ending force play. (Under baseball's rules, if the third out of an inning is made on a force play, any run which might have crossed the plate on that play, even if it occurred prior to the force, would not count.)

Leaving the basepath to join a game-winning celebration before touching second and removing the force was not uncommon in those days. The technical requirement that the base runner touch second in a game-winning situation was not often enforced, and umpires were not always vigilant in ensuring that second base was touched. In any event, seeing the base runner fail to touch second, the ever-alert Evers retrieved the ball and stepped on second. But his pleas to umpire Hank O'Day fell on deaf ears. O'Day apparently had not seen the route taken by the runner from first base and ruled that the run would stand.

The Cubs protested, but to no avail. Chance felt that it would be unlikely that he would ever see that same situation arise again. But the league told the umps to keep their eyes open for such situations in the future.[286] O'Day especially took note of the league directive, and later that month, the Cubs would benefit immeasurably from his diligence.

////

By September 18, the Cubs were in second place, facing a formidable uphill climb, now trailing the Giants by a full four and a half games with only sixteen games remaining. At that point, even Johnny Evers had doubts that the Cubs would be able to pull off a third straight pennant.[287] The upcoming schedule didn't promise any favors, either. The Cubs were looking at back-to-back doubleheaders on September 21 and 22 in two different cities, Philadelphia and New York.

The Cubs, however, won both games of the September 21 doubleheader in Philadelphia, reducing the Giants' lead to two games. The Cubs then faced the challenge of immediately jumping on a train after the long doubleheader, trying to get a decent night's sleep and playing another doubleheader, this time in New York the very next day to open a crucial four-game series.

Despite those obstacles, on the next day, September 22, the Cubs repeated their sweep of the day before, taking both games of the doubleheader in New York against the Giants. Three Finger Brown saved the game for Overall in the opener and was the winning pitcher in the second game. The two road doubleheader victories in two consecutive days in two different cities brought the Cubs to only one-half game behind the Giants.[288]

The next (third) game in the Cubs-Giants four-game series in New York was to be played on September 23. While most everyone considered that game to be big, no one had reason to expect that it would become the most controversial game in baseball history, featuring one of the wildest endings during one of the closest pennant races ever.

Chapter 2

SEPTEMBER 23, 1908

Merkle's Boneheaded Blunder

As was the case when the Cubs played the Pirates back on September 4, Hank O'Day was umpiring behind the plate for the September 23 contest between the Cubs and Giants. O'Day would play a key role in this game, especially in the end. Umpiring the bases was his partner, Bob Emslie.

The game began as a classic pitching duel between the Cubs' Jack Pfiester and the Giants' ace, Christy Mathewson. Both pitchers dominated in their performances that day, throwing shutout baseball for the first four innings. Tinker's solo homer in the fifth inning was the only dent the Cubs would make against Mathewson. Pfiester, who would pitch the entire game in pain with an injured tendon in his left throwing arm,[289] did not yield a run until the sixth, and that run was unearned, attributable to a two-base throwing error by Steinfeldt.

Going into the bottom of the ninth, the score was tied, 1–1. Afternoon sunlight was turning to dusk, and darkness would soon be setting in. This was likely the last inning that could be played that day. With one out, the Giants' Art Devlin singled to center. The next batter, "Moose" McCormick, grounded sharply to Evers, who threw to Tinker for the force on Devlin at second for the second out. Rookie Fred Merkle, in his first major league start, playing in place of the injured Fred Tenney, was the next batter. Merkle kept the inning alive by hitting a long single to right field, sending McCormick, with the potential winning run, all the way to third base.[290] As the next hitter, Al Bridwell, came to the plate with two outs and runners on the corners and the game at a possible tipping point, the crowd rose to its collective feet and roared in anticipation.[291]

Bridwell ripped a waist-high fastball from Pfiester up the middle so hard that it sent base umpire Emslie sprawling on his backside. Bridwell's clutch single to center field sent McCormick lumbering home with the apparent winning run. Bridwell appeared to be the hero. But his base hit would, ironically, be one he came to wish had never happened because of the anguish it would cause his teammate Fred Merkle.[292]

After Bridwell's hit, Giants players and thousands of fans spilled onto the field in a chaotic state of pandemonium, celebrating an apparent victory that would provide a huge shot in the arm for the team's pennant chances. The size of the crowd that stormed the field was enormous, and eventually, the entire playing surface was covered with fans.

Giants players on the field, while in a celebratory mood, made a dash for the safety of their clubhouse, which was located beyond the center-field fence, safe from the rampaging and mostly drunken hordes. Coincidentally, the fastest exit for fans in the Polo Grounds grandstands was also just beyond the center-field fence. Thousands of exiting fans headed, as usual, toward that exit. They were joined, however, by thousands of rowdy and rampaging fans also heading toward center field, but trying to touch or hug one of their heroes.

Seeing McCormick cross the plate, the crowd storming the field and his Giants teammates dashing to reach the safety of their center-field clubhouse, the inexperienced Merkle did what he had seen many other players do in the same situation. He joyously left the basepath and headed straight for the clubhouse without touching second base and removing the force out.

In the meantime, amid all the chaos with fans celebrating and players trying to escape, the savvy Evers was standing at second base screaming for Artie Hofman in center to throw him the ball. Evers had seen Merkle divert from his path. Hofman fired the ball to Evers at second to try to force Merkle. Then things became bizarre. First, Giants captain Mike Donlin, seeing Merkle stray from the basepath and realizing that the Cubs were seeking to force him at second, ran onto the field to try to chase down Merkle and alert him to touch second, but with no luck.

At the same time, Giants pitcher Joe "Iron Man" McGinty, who was coaching at third base, saw the same thing as Donlin. As his nickname suggests, McGinty was not one to be messed with. He had once operated a saloon and acted as his own bouncer. He was always known as a fighter. He didn't hesitate to verbally spar with the opposition, and often the verbal sparring escalated to full-scale brawling. In 1901, he was suspended for twelve days after physically assaulting umpire Tommy Connolly. He also engaged in a wild, on-field fistfight with Pittsburgh's Heinie Peitz in 1906, for which he was briefly jailed and eventually suspended for ten days.[293]

In any event, like Donlin, McGinty took off and ran onto the field through the delirious crowd. But unlike Donlin, he headed directly for second base. There, incredibly, amid the rampaging crowd on the field as darkness set in, McGinty attempted to intercept the throw from Hofman to Evers at second base!

After that, things became even more bizarre, and accounts of what occurred vary almost to a man. According to some

New York Giants' Fred Merkle. *Chicago History Museum.*

accounts, Tinker, Evers and possibly a third Cub then wrestled McGinty for the ball in the middle of the diamond, eventually taking it from McGinty. Evers then stepped on second for the force out on Merkle, who had never touched the base.[294] Other accounts say that McGinty won the wrestling match and rifled the game ball into the crowd, only to find that Evers somehow got hold of another ball.[295]

In reviewing accounts from Brown, Evers, Tinker and McGinty—all of which differed in some respects—the following is a plausible scenario. With McGinty trying to intercept Hofman's throw to second base, the ball hit Tinker in the back of the neck (as Tinker said) or on his shoulder (as Brown claimed). The ball then bounced away while McGinty and Cubs infielders scrambled for it. McGinty, however, picked up the ball and tried to throw it out of the park, but one of the Cubs, possibly Pfiester, grabbed his arm or hand in the act of throwing. That caused the ball to harmlessly land near third base, where fans, who had stormed the field, were standing. Steinfeldt went to pick it up but was beaten to the ball by a fan, whom Steinfeldt engaged, either by begging him for the ball or wrestling him for it. While Steinfeldt was so engaged with the fan, Cubs left-handed pitcher Floyd Kroh came by and slugged the fan. The wallop made the fan drop the ball. Steinfeldt picked it up. He may have brought the ball to Evers, who was standing on second base, or given it to Tinker, who got the ball over to Evers.[296]

Then, according to Evers, O'Day saw Evers standing on second with the ball while Merkle was making his dash for the clubhouse without touching second. O'Day called Merkle out and shouted that the run didn't count. O'Day then ran for his life through an enraged mob, which jostled and menaced him.[297] Of course, with so many differing accounts of what happened that day and the absence of any video to review, it is probable that we will never know what really happened.

Eyewitness accounts of O'Day's actions on that play also varied. Some accounts commended O'Day for his diligence. For example, the *Tribune* noted that, having grown wiser from his experience during the similar episode in Pittsburgh a few weeks before, on September 4, O'Day was alert for this situation.[298] Other accounts, however, are less flattering toward O'Day, saying that once McCormick crossed the plate, O'Day had already started to retire to the umpires' locker area behind home plate and could not have seen whether Merkle had touched second or what had happened between Evers and McGinty at second before eventually calling Merkle out.

In any event, after O'Day called Merkle out, there was still a large, chaotic—and by now confused—crowd on the field. With that, as well as darkness setting in, O'Day felt that the game could not be resumed. He ended the game and called it a "no contest."[299]

After the game, the Giants appealed the decision, claiming that the winning run had scored in the ninth. The Cubs appealed as well, arguing that the interference by the New York home crowd prevented the game from continuing, and thus the Giants should forfeit the game.

After the Cubs submitted their appeal, amid all the postgame confusion, Cubs owner Charles Murphy expressed optimism about the team's chances of winning the pennant. He further indicated that those chances would be even greater if the league upheld his appeal of the contest.[300] For his part, Chance said that he was glad the Cubs had filed an appeal after the similar incident in the Pirates game a few weeks before, because, according to Chance, it obviously made umpire O'Day more aware of the situation.[301]

##

Confusion about the events of the September 23 game continued into the next day, as the September 24 morning editions of the New York papers appeared to disregard O'Day's final call and printed the final score as 2–1 in favor of the Giants. That result was used in the standings published in the papers that morning. Furthermore, the league's slow and cautious handling of the appeals would only add to the confusion. The league, obviously hoping that the season would play out with the pennant decided by more than one game—thus rendering any appeal moot and making unnecessary any ruling from the league office—had not yet ruled on the appeals and would not do so for nearly two weeks.

Later that afternoon, the Cubs and Giants met again at the Polo Grounds for the final game of the series and their last scheduled face-to-face regular-season game. Fuming about what had taken place the day before, Giants fans were out for blood. They taunted the Chicago players, calling them "yellow dogs," "quitters" and "bribers of umpires." The Giants were not exactly restrained themselves. While McGraw and Evers engaged in a display of name-calling throughout the game, the Giants were more focused on umpire O'Day. For example, when O'Day took the field, the Giants' Bresnahan asked him if he should not be wearing a *C* on his shirt. That day, the Giants won the final game of the series and took a one-game lead.

After the series with New York, the Cubs moved across the East River to Brooklyn, where the atmosphere was more serene and far less combative, to battle the Superbas. On September 25, while the Cubs and Giants awaited a ruling on their respective appeals of the Merkle game, the Cubs' pennant chances were bolstered considerably as they took the first game against the Superbas and the Giants lost both games of a doubleheader.

The next day, September 26, Ed Reulbach added further fuel to the Cubs' pennant push. Chicago won, 5–0, in the first game, and Reulbach felt so confident afterward that he implored Chance to allow him to pitch the second game. Chance relented, and Reulbach and the Cubs prevailed, 3–0, in the nightcap. Reulbach had just thrown two complete-game shutouts in one day! Today, Reulbach remains the only pitcher in major league history to pitch complete-game doubleheader shutouts.[302]

By Sunday, October 4, the last day of the season for the Cubs and Pirates, all three teams remained alive in a three-way race for the pennant. That day, the Pirates came into West Side Grounds for one game to end the season. Pittsburgh had a half-game lead over the Cubs and could have eliminated Chicago with a victory. The Cubs, however, shellacked the Pirates, 5–2, eliminating the Bucs from the pennant race. The Cubs had won fourteen of their last sixteen, not counting two ties, to put themselves in the driver's seat to claim their third straight pennant.[303]

While the Cubs' season was over, the Giants still had three games to play with Boston, Monday through Wednesday, October 5–7. If the Giants won all three games, the Cubs and Giants would have identical records. In that case, under the National League constitution, a tie would be broken by a three-game postseason playoff in which each team would get at least one home game.

The Giants won the first two against Boston on October 5 and 6. Then, on the morning of the Giants' final game with Boston, October 7, the National League directors finally ruled on the appeals filed by both teams regarding the September 23 "Merkle" game. The league directors ruled that Merkle had been "reckless" in failing to touch second base and thus denied the Giants' appeal. Regarding the Cubs' appeal, the directors ruled that it would be "absurd" to order the Giants to forfeit the game because of the riotous crowd. What was most surprising, however, was that, although the league constitution required that the season end on Wednesday, October 7, the directors ruled that the season be extended one more day to replay the tie. The net result was that, regardless of whether the Giants beat Boston on October 7, the Cubs would speedily have to make the one-thousand-mile return trip to New York to replay the September 23 game at the Polo Grounds the next day, Thursday, October 8.[304]

The Giants defeated Boston on October 7. The Cubs and Giants had identical records. But instead of a three-game playoff series in which each team would have at least one home game, they would play just one game—their biggest "regular season" game ever. The pressure-packed, winner-take-all battle would, for all practical purposes, be the equivalent of a playoff game on the Cubs' enemy's home field on ridiculously short notice. Chicago was outraged but undaunted. They shook off what they considered an adverse and unjust ruling and were determined to win in New York.

Chapter 3

SHOWDOWN

The Playoff Game That Wasn't

For the Cubs, however, just getting to New York in a little over twenty-four hours to play the game posed a monumental logistical obstacle. The customary train trip to New York took twenty-eight hours, which would make the Cubs late in arriving for game time. The Cubs, therefore, booked, at significant additional expense, the fastest possible train, the 20th Century Limited, with the most powerful locomotive engine available. By doing so, the travel time to New York would be reduced to eighteen hours.[305]

The Cubs departed from LaSalle Street Station on the afternoon of October 7 to the cheers of about two hundred well-wishers. With the short notice, Johnny Kling, who was already back in Missouri when the league issued its ruling, was fortunate to get back to Chicago in the nick of time to catch the train just before it was ready to depart, much to the relief of the Peerless Leader. The 20th Century Limited would arrive in Manhattan at 9:30 a.m., just hours ahead of the midafternoon playoff game. After a less-than-optimal night of sleep aboard the train, the Cubs would then have just a few hours to regain their playing legs. Despite all these obstacles, the Cubs were confident and ready. On the train to New York, the Peerless Leader told reporters, "Whoever heard of the Cubs losing a game that they had to have?"[306]

Manager Chance indicated that he would go with the same lineup he had used in the September 23 game, with Pfiester "the Giant Killer" on the hill. Chance had the option of going with either Pfiester or his ace, Brown. He went with Pfiester but had Brown available just in case. McGraw, of course, would go with Mathewson, who had won thirty-seven games that season. McGraw, who could not tolerate mental errors, had only one change to his lineup. Merkle, whose baserunning debacle on September 23 cost the Giants the victory, would not be in the starting lineup.[307] In fact, for his mistake in that game, Merkle was eventually given, and would forever bear, the moniker "Bonehead" Merkle.

Tremendous excitement in New York preceded the playoff game. According to the *New York Sun*, "No such gathering of hopeful enthusiasts ever looked at a baseball game before and hoped against hope for a home team to win."[308] The *New York Times* reported that "there is no record of a sporting event that stirred New York as did the game of yesterday. No crowd so big ever was moved to a field of contest as was moved yesterday. Perhaps never in the history of a great city, since the days of Rome and its arena contests has a people been pitched to such a key of excitement as was New York 'fandom' yesterday."[309]

Tremendous pregame excitement pervaded Chicago as well. The Cubs-Giants game occupied the thoughts of most Chicagoans that day, and crowds gathered around telegraph lines in hopes of catching the latest update from the Polo Grounds.[310] Meanwhile, at the Polo Grounds, prodigious crowds were arriving. Some fans arrived as early as daybreak. By 10:30 a.m., more than four hours before game time, seven thousand fans were at the gate, and the police who were there to control the crowd were simply swept aside. By 12:45 p.m., more than two hours before game time, all seats and standing-room space in the park had been taken. That did not deter men and boys from attempting various means of sneaking into the stadium. Some even scaled a fifteen-foot fence topped with barbed wire to get in.

Those who could not get into the Polo Grounds tried to view the contest from nearby Coogan's Bluff, which overlooked the ballpark. Others climbed trees or light poles or tried to watch from a nearby elevated train platform. Train service was halted because fans were sitting on the tracks. One fan fell from the platform and was killed. The *New York Times* reflected the crowd's relative indifference to the tragedy by casually noting, "His vacant place was quickly filled."[311]

Scalpers made a fortune selling tickets outside the stadium, but the buyers soon realized that their overpriced tickets were useless, because they could not get into the stadium.[312] If the September 23 Merkle game had the wildest ending for a baseball game in the Deadball Era, the October 8 showdown was the most anticipated of that era. Eventually, while the Polo Grounds' seating capacity was sixteen thousand, more than forty thousand people would see the game from both within and outside of the stadium.

For their pregame warmups, the Cubs entered the field from the clubhouse one or two players at a time. Each Cub player who took the field received a loud and rude reception from the boisterous and partisan crowd that had taken their seats hours before the start of the game. The spectators jeered and heaped vitriol on the Chicago players. Yet the Cubs swaggered as they entered the field, almost strutting with an air of confidence, seemingly undisturbed by the verbal abuse. No Cubs player, however, received more verbal abuse that day than Manager Frank Chance. Nonetheless, even the New York writers marveled at how the Peerless Leader carried himself, with great professionalism and dignity, his chin up, acting as if he were oblivious to the indignities hurled his way.[313]

The verbal abuse came not just from the fans but from the Giants themselves, and it did not stop once the game started. "Iron Man" McGinty tried to insult and goad Chance into a fight. The Giants likely strategized that if a fight ensued between the two, and both got kicked out of the game, the Giants would not miss McGinty, who was not playing, but the Cubs would definitely miss Chance, who *was* playing.

McGinty did everything he could to provoke Chance. While the Cubs were five minutes into their batting practice, McGinty grabbed a bat and tried to kick the Cubs off the field, cutting their batting practice short. The Cubs objected, and Chance and McGinty "bristled" against each other.[314] McGinty trash-talked Chance, stepped on his toes and even spat on him.[315] With the game so important, however, the Peerless Leader, against his natural inclination to brawl, absorbed the abuse for the good of his team and did not fight.[316]

From the outset of the game, the Cubs' "Giant Killer" just didn't have it. Pfiester lacked his usual control, and the Giants struck for one run in the first inning to take the lead. Before the first inning was over, Chance had seen enough. He removed Pfiester and went to Mordecai Brown in relief. Brown was up to the task, closing out the Giants in the first with no more damage. Brown then got all the support he needed in the Cubs' half of the third inning.

With the Giants still leading, 1–0, Joe Tinker led off the third inning against Mathewson. For the Cubs, Tinker was the right man to come to bat at the right time. In 1908, Tinker had emerged as a team leader. Playing in all 157 games, Tinker batted .266 and led Chicago in hits (146), triples (14), home runs (6), RBIs (68) and slugging percentage (.391).[317] From 1906

On-field dispute during the October 8, 1908 Cubs versus Giants game at Polo Grounds. *Library of Congress.*

on, after Tinker went on to use a longer bat to meet Mathewson's deadly low, outside curveball, Tinker practically owned Matty. Tinker batted .364 against him in 1907 and over .400 against him in 1908.[318] Tinker so often got the better of Mathewson that in his 1912 book *Pitching in a Pinch*, Mathewson described him as "the worst man I have to face in the National League."[319]

With that history of Tinker and Mathewson as background and the Cubs trailing, 1–0, in the third, Matty fired his first pitch of the inning. Tinker was ready, and he ripped a long triple. Whether Mathewson was tiring from having pitched in nine of the last fifteen Giants games of the 1908 season is not clear. Tinker's triple, however, jump-started a decisive four-run inning for the Cubs—an inning that included an RBI single by Kling, an intentional walk, an RBI double by Schulte and a two-run double by Chance, giving the Cubs a 4–1 lead.[320]

After that, Brown had his way with the Giants, dominating them the rest of the way. He appeared stronger as the game went on, retiring the New Yorkers in order in the eighth and ninth. When Bridwell grounded out to Tinker for the final out, the Cubs had defeated Mathewson and the Giants, 4–2, and won their third consecutive National League pennant.

While the New York fans mercilessly verbally berated Chance during the game, there was no physical violence until after the game. When the final out was made, Chance made his way toward the Cubs' clubhouse, where a crowd of Giants fans awaited him in the nearby spectator seating section. One fan pulled out a soda-water bottle and hurled it at Chance, striking him in the neck, where he was hurt "painfully." Pfiester was struck by another thrown bottle, but he suffered only a slight bruise.[321] The Cubs "made it to the dressing room and barricaded the door."[322] But that didn't stop stones from crashing through the windows while the players were dressing.[323] According to Mordecai Brown, "Outside, wild men were yelling for our blood—really. As the mob got bigger, the police came up and formed a line across the door. We read the next day that the cops had to pull their revolvers to hold them back. I couldn't say as to that. We weren't sticking our heads out to see."[324]

After the game, the New York media was far more gracious and complimentary to the Cubs than to the New York "fandom." For example, according to the *New York Evening Mail*, "Chicago won the championship because it was coming to them. It is the cleanest, fastest, surest baseball organization ever joined together. That's why they are three-time champions and that's why they will again cop the world's title from Detroit."[325]

In the meantime, after word of the Cubs' victory reached Chicago, revelers packed State Street, ringing bells and waving Cubs flags. Newsboys hawking the latest editions with the story of the victory only added to the din, and their newspapers were quickly bought up. Celebrations popped up in restaurants and cafés and in L trains and streetcars. The Cubs were basically the only topic of conversation in the city that day.[326]

The players had little time to celebrate. After their breakneck train journey to New York with less than optimum rest, and then winning the deciding game of the pennant race in front of a hostile, even violent crowd, the team then had to make another train trip, this time to Detroit. It would be a World Series rematch with the American League champion Tigers. The first game was to start in just two days.

Chapter 4

THE WORLD SERIES

The 1908 Cubs had demonstrated in the regular season that, while they had "an offense without stars," they had "a lot of aggressiveness. They had quick-thinking players at a time when outsmarting your opponent was a big difference. They hit and ran, took the extra base on hits and outs. When they needed to make a run, they were experts at finding a way to score."[327] Possibly most important, they had dominant pitching. For example, in the 1908 regular season, Brown went 29-9 with an incredible ERA of 1.47, and Reulbach went 24-7 with an ERA of 2.03. With good reason, these Cubs certainly didn't lack confidence and talent, and they boasted about sweeping the series from the Tigers this time.

In Game One, however, played on October 10 in Detroit, the Cubs had their backs to the wall. With Chicago trailing 6–5 in the ninth, the Tigers fans were smelling blood. The Cubs, however, rallied with six consecutive hits to score five runs off reliever Ed Summers. The key hit was a bases-loaded single by Solly Hofman. Chicago went on to win Game One by a score of 10–6.[328]

Game Two moved to Chicago and West Side Grounds the next day, October 11. This time, the Cubs won rather easily, as Overall threw a complete game and the Cubs hit "Wild Bill" Donovan hard. The final was Cubs 6, Tigers 1, in front of 17,780 fans.

In the first two games of the series, the Tigers' young star, Ty Cobb, had been relatively quiet. In Game Three, however, played again in Chicago, Cobb came alive. He rapped three singles and a double in five at-bats to support Tigers pitcher George Mullin, who threw a complete game. The Tigers won their first World Series game against the Cubs in two years by a score of 8–3.

Despite playing at home in Game Four, the Tigers offense once again went dormant. Brown threw a complete-game shutout, and the Cubs went on to win, 3–0. After that, the consensus among most baseball people was that the series was over. Judging by the attendance at the next game in Detroit, the consensus apparently included Tigers fans.

For Game Five, only 6,210 fans showed up at Bennett Field. Furthermore, most were Cubs fans who had made the trip by train from Chicago. In the first inning, the Cubs strung together three hits to score the only run they would need. Chance drove in Evers with a single. In the Tigers' half of the inning, Overall struck out four batters, setting a new major league record. One of those strikeouts involved a dropped third strike in the dirt that eluded Kling and allowed Claude Rossman to reach first. In the fifth, the Cubs scored again, as Evers doubled to left center to score Kling. News accounts of the game indicated that the Tigers fought desperately, but their bats were quiet. Overall threw a complete-game shutout, allowing only three hits, and the Cubs won, 2–0.

The Cubs became the first team to win back-to-back world championships. Chicago pitchers held the Tigers to a .203 batting average for the World Series and shut the Tigers out over the last nineteen innings. Frank Chance hit .421, and Wildfire Schulte hit .399.

After the game's final out was recorded by Kling catching a foul pop-up, passionate Cubs fans who had made the journey to Detroit by train let loose with a thunderous, joyous yell from the grandstand. Meanwhile, the Tigers graciously trotted over to the Cubs' bench trying to congratulate them. But the passionate Chicago fans stormed the field, straining to reach and celebrate with their heroes as the Cubs suddenly dashed off, seeking the safety of their clubhouse.[329] Those Cubs fans likely assumed that, after the team's three consecutive pennants and two consecutive World Series championships, title celebrations might become an annual, almost routine, event. Those fans, however, could not have possibly imagined that not one of them would live long enough to see the team win their next World Series (in 2016).

◊◊◊

A few evenings later, on October 16, 1908, entertainer and "Yankee Doodle Dandy" George M. Cohan was in Chicago, appearing in a play, *The Yankee Prince*. Cohan invited the Cubs to a restaurant called Rector's to celebrate their repeating as world champions. Tinkers, Evers and Chance were there, as were the Sheckards and the Steinfeldts.[330]

Cohan, however, did not invite Cubs owner Charles W. Murphy. Despite the team's two world championships, Murphy was incredibly unpopular with Cubs fans, players, the manager and many of the other National League owners. Some of his detractors called him "cheap" and not always honest. Many fans were upset at the high price of World Series tickets charged by Murphy, as well as the poor choice of seats. In fact, thousands of tickets for World Series games at West Side Grounds were not sold despite the high demand. This benefited the scalpers, who could sell tickets at a higher price. But it hurt the average fan, who wanted to see the ball games, and it hurt the players, whose "take" from the series depended on ticket sales.

The public suspected that Murphy was colluding with scalpers, although Murphy claimed that no one fought scalpers harder than Cubs management. He claimed that due to the short period between the team's playoff win in New York and the beginning of the World Series, problems understandably arose. There was just not enough time to get ready for the series and make all tickets available for the fans.

Murphy likely recalled how in 1907 he had hosted, and been the toast of, an elegant banquet at the Waldorf-Astoria honoring his world champion Cubs. But just one year later he was not invited to the banquet in honor of his 1908 champions. Understandably, Murphy did not take Cohan's snub well. He wrote a letter to the *Tribune*, concluding, "Rome was not built in a day, and it takes time even in Chicago to get ready for a World Series." When Murphy made that claim, he clearly was referring to the fact that he could have used a few more days to make ticket arrangements and better accommodate his fan base for the World Series. A century later, *Tribune* columnist Mike Downey wrote that Murphy "was right. It has taken the Cubs [as of 2007] nearly 99 years to get ready [for a World Series]."[331]

According to Downey and Grant DePorter of Harry Caray's Restaurant, the snub of Murphy in 1908 began the true curse of the Cubs, one in which a billy goat played a part, but only a small part, in an even more elaborate pre-2016 curse. The goat that was denied access to a Wrigley Field game in 1945 was named Murphy. Bob Murphy was the name of the New York Mets' announcer when a black cat crossed in front of the Cubs' dugout in Shea Stadium in 1969. Jack Murphy Stadium was the ballpark in San Diego where the Cubs folded in the 1984 playoffs.[332] Moreover, the Mets slugger who tormented the Cubs in their 2015 National League Championship Series debacle was Daniel Murphy. It appears that the pre-2016 Cubs may have been vexed by their own distinctive version of "Murphy's Law." Considering all that, it seems poetic justice that one of the prominent watering holes where Cubs fans have drowned their sorrows over the years is Murphy's Bleachers.

Chapter 5

THE 1908 FIRST WARD BALL

It's a lollapalooza....Chicago ain't no sissy town.
—*Hinky Dink Kenna, following the 1908 First Ward Ball*

At about the same time in October that the Cubs were hosting their 1908 championship celebration at Rector's—without owner Charles Murphy—ministers and reformers in Chicago were busy trying to head off another, but far more controversial, celebration. As the time for the annual First Ward Ball approached, they feared another night of depravity and debauchery, much like that during the 1907 First Ward Ball.

In October 1908, the ministers and reformers vigorously issued a resolution condemning the event and demanded that Mayor Fred Busse refrain from issuing a liquor license for the Coliseum. Other reform groups soon joined the protest. A lawsuit was even filed seeking to enjoin the holding of the event. Nonetheless, Coughlin and Kenna won the day. The motion for injunctive relief was denied, and the liquor license was approved. The 1908 First Ward Ball had received the official go-ahead.

On the evening of the ball, December 14, thousands of attendees waiting outside for the Coliseum doors to open were joined on Wabash and Fifteenth by thousands more protesters and onlookers. The onlookers had no intention of attending the ball. They had come to see what was happening and who was attending, or they were drawn by the excitement generated by the event. The crowds were so large that they stopped traffic outside the Coliseum. When the doors were thrown open, the rowdy throngs

Chicago Coliseum, 1907. *Chicago History Museum.*

of attendees surged forward. The number seeking entrance greatly exceeded the capacity of the Coliseum, and the 100 police officers and 150 ushers were quickly overwhelmed and were unable to maintain control.[333]

Those in the unruly crowd had no interest in waiting in line for drinks. Waiters and bartenders watched helplessly as champagne and beer were ripped away from their trays and bars without being paid for. After the first twelve thousand people were inside, the police closed the gates for fear of overcrowding.[334] This, however, did not deter many in the crowd. Thousands more stormed the exit doors until the police could finally close them from the inside. Finally, around 10:00 p.m., some semblance of order was restored—enough so that, to the delight of Coughlin and Kenna, money could finally be collected for drinks.

According to the *Tribune*, the ball was attended by nearly every criminal and unsavory character in Chicago.[335] Not anxious to have the city's politicians seen cavorting with criminals, and concerned that photos of indecently clad women might fall into the hands of reformers, Coughlin prohibited photographers from attending. When Coughlin caught a photographer taking a photo, Bathhouse thrashed the unlucky man. Later, in court, Coughlin preposterously claimed in his defense that he believed that, when the photographer's flash powder went off, the man was shooting at Coughlin in an assassination attempt.[336]

As was the case in the 1907 First Ward Ball, incredible quantities of champagne and beer were consumed—over thirty thousand quarts of beer and ten thousand bottles of champagne. Fights and brawls broke out repeatedly, and with nearly twenty thousand revelers jammed into the Coliseum, if someone were to pass out, there would be little room to fall. Inside and outside, chaos reigned. While those outside struggled madly to get in, those stuck in the chaos inside tried to get out.[337] The air inside was thick with cigar smoke. That, together with the severely crowded conditions and the over-imbibing, which was the general rule of the day, caused some women to faint. Because of the overcrowding, there was no way to make a path to get them outside, so those women had to be passed hand-to-hand over the heads of people to the exits, with men yelling, "Gangway, dame fainted!"[338]

Just before midnight, the Everleigh sisters and their group of prostitutes grabbed the spotlight when they arrived. Their arrival caused thousands of men outside to try to storm the building to get a glimpse of the women. Afterward and throughout the night, prostitutes mingled, and even more intimately socialized, with politicians and other members of Chicago's elite. At midnight, while five thousand people remained outside still trying to gain admission,[339] the "Grand March" took place. Coughlin's Grand March was a massive, indoor procession of thousands of members of the city's underworld— pimps, prostitutes, gamblers, thieves, women dressed in scandalous slit-cut dresses and bathing suits and men dressed as women. (In fact, one of the first Chicago references to what we refer to today as "cross-dressers" or "drag queens" appeared in accounts of the event.)

The participants in the Grand March were led by the extravagantly dressed Coughlin, who wore a red sash and lavender tie. Joining Coughlin were the Everleigh sisters, who had arrived in time for the march, and their band of prostitutes. Those in the Grand March strutted and snaked their way in a wild dance line through the Coliseum, cheered on by thousands of spectators.

Then, after the midnight Grand March, things really got interesting. As Coughlin was known to say of the ball, "Things don't get good until 3 a.m." By then, young, "scantily dressed" women, some "hardly out of their girlhood days," danced drunkenly and provocatively with drunken men. The actions of the men were "highly questionable," and many of the men appeared to be old enough to be the girls' grandfathers.[340] Young "beardless boys" were often seen in the company of "old and cunning women."[341] Couples snuck into quiet corners of the basement or annex to cavort more intimately. The most notorious orgy in Chicago history finally ended at around 5:00 a.m.[342]

In the end, although there were many police officers present, only one conviction resulted from the ball. A man was convicted for getting in without paying for a ticket. Coughlin and Kenna earned about $50,000 from the 1908 First Ward Ball. Kenna exclaimed, "It's a lollapalooza….Chicago ain't no sissy town."[343]

PART VI

1909

[The groundhog's] *prognostications are invariably correct,*
which cannot be said of the men whom the government pays big wages
to dope out the weather for us.
—Bathhouse Coughlin's unsuccessful January 1909 pitch to the Chicago City
Council as part of his "pet measure" to declare Groundhog Day
a legal city holiday[344]

Chapter 1

104 WINS...BUT THE CUBS FALL SHORT

For the Cubs, early 1909 would bring discord. For example, in January, Johnny Evers married Helen Fitzgibbons, from his hometown of Troy, New York. (Newspapers referred to her as "Helen of Troy.") After the wedding, Evers stunned reporters and his teammates by announcing that he was going on a honeymoon and wouldn't return until June, two months after the start of the baseball season. Whether Evers was serious or just having some fun, no one could tell.

Another example is that, soon after the 1908 season ended, Chance and Murphy argued over team control, and Chance made clear from his offseason retreat in California that he was considering not coming back to the Cubs. The enmity between the two seemed as much personal as business. By late January, the dispute between Murphy and Chance had become so great that Chance and his wife were contemplating returning to Chicago, selling their home and Chance's stock in the Cubs and settling down in an orange grove in California. But by early February, the rift between the two was resolved through the brokering of *Tribune* reporter Harvey Woodruff, a friend of Chance working out of Los Angeles. According to Chance, Woodruff "pointed out several errors in my line of reasoning, and several exchanges of telegrams and phone calls brought the whole matter to a close."[345]

On February 6, when Chance wrote a letter "to the baseball fans of Chicago" stating that he would return to the team for the 1909 season, all of Cubs fandom cheered, for it seemed that a fourth straight NL pennant was all but assured. Murphy himself expressed the opinion of most fans when he wrote, "Chance's return means another flag."[346]

Those flag chances took a big hit in March, however, when Johnny Kling abruptly announced that he was quitting the Cubs, citing a dispute with Murphy. Earlier the prior year, Kling had wanted to buy a pool hall in Cincinnati from the owner of the Reds, but Murphy squelched the deal, taking the position that the Reds owner was "tampering" with Kling.[347] Kling had spent the offseason following the 1908 campaign winning the world billiards championship, and he then invested in a billiards hall in Kansas City. Upset with Murphy, Kling was content to stay in Kansas City to tend to his business interests and play pool.[348]

Kling's quitting would deprive the Cubs of probably the best catcher in baseball, with Pat Moran, the team's backup catcher, assuming the starting role. Chance, however, had confidence in Moran: "I consider Kling the greatest catcher in baseball today. Next to Kling, I consider Moran the best.…The Cubs are strong enough to win without Kling and Chicago fans need lose no sleep over this desertion."[349]

There was, however, even more cause for concern. For one thing, Jimmy Slagle, the Cubs' starting center fielder and leadoff hitter during the three pennant-winning seasons, had retired after the 1908 season. Furthermore, Evers still had not shown up for spring training workouts. He eventually missed some regular season games, but his absence was relatively brief, as he was able to play in 127 of the club's 153 games that season.[350] More seriously, however, Frank Chance suffered a broken shoulder and missed more than 50 games in 1909.[351] Notwithstanding the best efforts of Pat Moran behind the plate, Kling indeed would be missed.

Despite all those obstacles, the Cubs won 104 games in 1909. That was truly a magnificent accomplishment. The Cubs would never again surpass that win total in a single season, although they equaled it in 1910. Even the 2016 world champion Cubs, despite dominating the National League from the start of the season to the finish, won only 103 games—and in a season that was 8 games longer. Nonetheless, without Kling and with the injury to Chance, the 1909 Cubs' achievement of 104 wins was still not enough to win their fourth consecutive pennant.

While some commentators cite Kling's absence as the reason for the Cubs' inability to repeat in 1909, Joe Tinker believed that the loss of Kling for the entire season did not hurt the team as much as the loss of Frank Chance to injury for more than 50 games, noting that the Cubs' infield just didn't function as efficiently without Chance at first base.[352] That year, the Pirates, led by Honus Wagner, won 110 games, finishing with an impressive 110-42 record and winning the NL pennant. The Cubs finished second, their 104 victories remaining the most for any second-place team in league history.

There would be no World Series appearance for the Cubs that October as there had been the previous three years. But the team was still busy that October. First, they captured the city championship by prevailing over the White Sox in the annual postseason City Series. Later that month, the Cubs took on semipro teams, as the lure of earning extra cash apparently lessened the sting of having lost to the semipro Logan Squares in 1906. One of the teams the Cubs played was an all-Black semipro team, almost unheard of at the time.

Chapter 2

POSTSEASON CLASH WITH THE LELAND GIANTS

In response to the exclusion of Black players from Major League Baseball prior to 1947, when Jackie Robinson joined the Dodgers, all-Black ball clubs and leagues were formed. They can be characterized as somewhere between the semipro and professional levels, and the quality of play by many of the players was on a par or better than that of their major league counterparts.

One of the top all-Black Chicago teams in the early twentieth century was the Leland Giants. In 1907, they had signed a young pitcher from Texas named "Rube" Foster, so nicknamed because once, pitching in an exhibition, Foster had beaten the legendary Philadelphia A's pitcher "Rube" Waddell. After that, Foster took Waddell's nickname.[353] Foster became the best Black pitcher in the country. The 1907 Leland Giants finished with an incredible 110-10 record, including 48 straight wins.[354] They took the pennant in the Chicago Baseball League.[355]

By 1909, an integrated, six-team, semipro City League had been formed, including the Logan Squares, the Gunthers, a team formed by Cap Anson, a Milwaukee team and the Leland Giants. The Giants were the only Black team in the City League. By this time, Foster was managing the Leland Giants. The 1909 Giants featured major league–quality Black players, including Andrew "Jap" Payne in right field, pitcher Walter "the Georgia Rabbit" Ball and catcher James "Pete" Booker. The league also featured pitcher Bill Gatewood, who later taught the legendary Satchel Paige his famous "hesitation pitch" and otherwise went on to develop Paige as a pitcher.[356]

Leland Giants pitcher Rube Foster. *Chicago History Museum.*

In 1909, the Leland Giants finished 31-9 and won the City League pennant. Ironically, the all-Black Giants beat out the white team fielded by Cap Anson—the same Anson who decades before had refused to play with a Black player and allegedly triggered the unofficial ban on Blacks in Major League Baseball. After the City League season was completed, an October 10, 1909 article in the *Tribune* proclaimed that Leland's team had such talent that "at least five of them would be in the major leagues if white."[357]

After the 1909 regular season, Foster challenged the Cubs to an October three-game postseason series. The Leland Giants played well, but the Cubs were able to sweep the series, winning three close games—two by just one run. Mordecai Brown pitched and won the first and third games for the Cubs.[358] Foster pitched the second game for the Giants, who took a 5–2 lead into the ninth but lost, 6–5.[359]

Chapter 3

"GYPSY" SMITH'S MARCH
ROCKS THE LEVEE

By mid-October 1909, at about the time when the Cubs–Leland Giants series was taking place, business in the Levee District was better than ever. Bordellos, panel houses, peep shows, saloons, gambling establishments and burlesque houses continued to flourish with little city government interference. On the other hand, reformers were livid over the degeneracy that had occurred at the 1908 First Ward Ball and that had been taking place in the Levee in general. They would continuously mount challenges to the corruption and depravity that had been the hallmark of the First Ward.

That month, one such challenge was mounted by a prominent and respected British evangelist, Rodney "Gypsy" Smith, who had amassed an impressive evangelical following in Chicago. He had visited the Levee District, was appalled by what he saw and decided that action was necessary. He announced plans for a rally and march on the Levee.[360]

On October 18, 1909, with the annual First Ward Ball less than two months away, Smith convened a daytime revival meeting at the Seventh Regiment Armory attended by some two thousand of his followers. Inside the Armory, Smith led the throng in prayer and hymns. He stoked the crowd by railing against the vices of the Levee District and the corrupt politicians who allowed the vice to stand. He then walked out of the Armory toward the Levee District with thousands of his followers in tow. A marching band accompanied the throng, which caught the attention of thousands of others who either lined the streets as spectators or joined the growing and marching throng. Smith and his followers occasionally stopped in front of a vice establishment, sang a hymn and knelt in the streets, offering a short prayer. Many of the bystanders, accustomed to the sordid status quo of the Levee, wondered what this march was hoping to accomplish. This was Chicago, after all! But Smith's followers continued their march through the district, decrying the city's crime and corruption and praying for the eradication of the sin and vice of the Levee. According to police estimates, the crowd eventually grew to fifty thousand people.[361]

While the march was proceeding, the proprietors of Levee establishments kept a low profile, staying mostly out of sight, with drapes drawn, doors shut and lights dimmed. The working girls either disappeared or changed into street clothes. Little if any evidence of vice activity could be seen during the march. But as the march died down and night settled in, the district came to life. It was as if a switch had been flipped. Lights were turned back on, doors were thrown open and the working girls returned to serving their customers. Many of the spectators who had come down to witness the rally were intrigued enough to stay and patronize the Levee's brothels, gambling halls and saloons. Indeed, with the huge crowd that had attended the march, there were plenty of new prospective customers for the bordellos and other houses of sin to serve. Even reform-minded marchers could be found in some of the Levee's establishments, including many of the impressionable young men who had come to the Levee for the first time to participate in the march. Many gave in to curiosity and temptation and stayed to sample the unholy pleasures the Levee offered. As a result, instead of shutting down Levee businesses as originally intended, Gypsy Smith's march provided businesses with one of their most profitable nights ever! Tongue-in-cheek, Minna Everleigh said that she was glad to get the business but sorry to see that so many clean young men had been exposed to life in the Levee.[362]

The march had no immediate adverse effect on the Levee, and business continued unabated in the short run. But Smith's march lit a spark for advocates of reform, and unlike in previous years, Mayor Fred Busse refused to issue a liquor license for the 1909 ball. That prompted Coughlin to write his shortest poem:

> *No ball;*
> *That's all.*[363]

Instead of hosting a ball in 1909, Coughlin and Kenna tried their luck at hosting a non-alcoholic concert, but that did not go over well. Police were present at the concert to make sure there was no alcohol or rowdiness, and fewer than three thousand people came. The First Ward Ball had seen its last day. Two years later, reformers would have their day. In 1911, the Levee was shut down.

Chapter 4

A CITY PLAN COMES TOGETHER

Make no little plans; they have no magic to stir men's blood
and probably themselves will not be realized.
—attributed to Daniel Burnham[364]

After years of planning and politicking, Daniel Burnham and co-author Edward H. Bennett's Plan of Chicago (the "Plan") was finally unveiled and presented to the city on July 4, 1909. The Plan was a 164-page document vividly illustrated in watercolors that clearly articulated a bold vision: "Within the lifetime of persons now living," Chicago would become "a greater City than any existing at the present time."[365] More important, it also contained far-sighted proposals intended to meet the needs anticipated from the realization of that vision.

The Plan was Burnham's response to Chicago's "half Century of explosive—yet haphazard—growth."[366] It called for an integrated planning approach to nearly all parts of the city and even the surrounding areas to alleviate traffic congestion and promote business. It also included proposals to beautify the city. To Burnham, a proponent of the subsequent City Beautiful movement, beauty in the urban setting was not only good for the average citizen, it was also good for local business. A beautiful city would "attract the upper class to work and spend money" and eliminate "vices and other unsavory behavior," especially among the lower classes.[367]

The Plan's combined integrated planning approach and emphasis on beautification had its most profound and lasting impact on the lakefront.

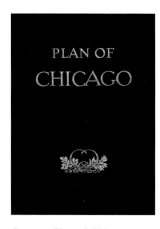

Cover to Plan of Chicago, 1909. *Chicago History Museum.*

At the time of the Plan's publication, much of the lakefront was subject to private control and not accessible to the public. Burnham's Plan proposed creating landfill to build more lakefront park space. By the 1920s and 1930s, Northerly Island—the future site of the 1933–34 World's Fair, the site of Meigs Field after World War II and the current site for summer concerts—was being built per the Plan. So was Burnham Park and Promontory Point. Moreover, by the 1950s, landfill had nearly tripled the size of Lincoln Park from what it had been at the time of the Plan.[368] As a result of the Plan, the lakefront ultimately consisted of "an unbroken string of lakefront parks"[369] that became home to beaches, harbors, lagoons and recreational areas.

The Plan improved the city's roads and bridges and alleviated congestion. It led to the double-decking of Wacker Drive and portions of Michigan Avenue, providing lower levels for trucks, wagons and commercial traffic while easing congestion on the upper level for consumers and lighter vehicles.

To win city approval, the planners met with the mayor, corporation counsel and, showing that they were willing to meet with anyone, even First Ward aldermen Coughlin and Kenna in an outreach effort. That meeting was not entirely surprising, as Burnham and Bathhouse always had a good relationship. Burnham's son Dan Jr. once said:

> *Bathhouse John was an old friend and admirer of my father, and he had a lot of charm, as all successful politicians must have. When I came on the stage, he extended this friendship to me and for many years he helped me out with political favors….Among his string of racehorses, he had one named "Dan Burnham" for my father….I put a bet one day at Arlington Park on "Dan Burnham" and watched the nag finish last.*[370]

Burnham's presentation and vision of the city's future resonated with Bathhouse John, who later exhorted the city to find the funding necessary to make Burnham's proposed improvements. Coughlin then made a speech in which he charged that if the city could not come up with the funding, it was "a city of pikers and deserved to take a back seat."[371]

While Burnham had his supporters, he was not devoid of opposition. In April 1907, U.S. Army engineer Colonel W.H. Bixby wrote to the governor opposing the development of lakefront parks, instead advocating for the building of more warehouses, piers and docks along the shore. He assumed that they would all be necessary to meet the needs of businesses in the central business district that would be receiving goods by ship. Eventually, it was decided that trains, not ships, were the future and that Calumet Harbor on the far South Side would be sufficient to meet the needs of the city in receiving goods arriving by ship.[372]

The Plan also addressed the needs of the citizens on the city's outskirts. It provided forest preserves to ring the city along its perimeter, providing more open spaces and offering places for recreation to city-dwellers who lacked easy access to the lakefront parks.

//////

Not only did the Plan capture the imagination of Chicagoans, it also attracted the attention of President William Howard Taft, successor to Theodore Roosevelt. The new president traveled to Chicago to see the Plan's drawings on September 16, 1909. That, however, was not the only reason Taft traveled to Chicago. He was a huge baseball fan, and his half-brother, Charles Taft, retained an interest in the Cubs. That same day, the president also visited West Side Grounds to watch a game between the Cubs and the Giants. He received a warm reception from the capacity crowd. The park was decked out with flags and bunting for his visit. Bands played, and the crowds cheered.[373]

President Taft was a large, heavy man weighing approximately three hundred pounds. After sitting through the first six and one-half innings, his joints were stiff. Between the halves of the seventh inning, he rose to stretch, and those around him dutifully followed suit.[374] While according to baseball lore the tradition of the "seventh-inning stretch" was started by President Taft on opening day the following year, 1910, in Pittsburgh, Taft's 1909 "stretch" at West Side Grounds predated the purported first seventh-inning stretch. In fairness, researchers have uncovered accounts of earlier versions of the seventh-inning stretch going back to 1869, and the exact origin of the tradition remains unsettled.

////

Despite the great interest shown by Chicagoans and even the president of the United States in Burnham's Plan for Chicago, not all of the Plan was implemented, and the City Beautiful movement had become disfavored among architects and city planners.

Later, in the twenty-first century, the City Beautiful movement underwent a resurrection of sorts, illustrated most vividly by the construction of Chicago's Millennium Park, located between Michigan Avenue and the lakefront near the Loop.[375] There, Chicagoans and tourists alike can enjoy beautiful gardens, walking paths, lakefront views, cutting-edge architecture and design, fountains and restaurants—all steps from the Loop. In some ways, Millennium Park is a modern extension of Burnham's Plan of Chicago.

What the Plan of Chicago did *not* contain were these words, long associated with the Plan and often attributed to Burnham: "Make no little plans. They have no magic to stir men's blood." It is not clear when, where or if Burnham actually stated or wrote those words, but the Plan of Chicago was no little plan.[376]

In calling on Daniel Burnham to design a Plan for the City of Chicago, the city's civic and business leaders had acted with energy, confidence and imagination. Unlike the citizens of San Francisco after their earthquake, Chicagoans did not allow themselves to be ruled by expedience. Unlike the city of St. Louis, which was content in the nineteenth century to wait for greatness to happen, Chicago's far-sighted leaders prized action and innovation and were willing to substantially go along with the vision for the city put forward by Daniel Burnham. Today, Chicagoans enjoy the benefits.

PART VII

1910

Chapter 1

TINKER TO EVERS TO CHANCE

At the beginning of the 1910 baseball season, the eyes of Chicago baseball were focused on the White Sox, as Charles Comiskey unveiled his brand-new, state-of-the-art "Baseball Palace" known as Comiskey Park. Made of steel and concrete, it opened one year after Shibe Park in Philadelphia debuted the first steel-and-concrete ballpark. Before then, all ballparks were made of wood. Built on the site of a former city dump, Comiskey Park would be the home of the White Sox for eighty years.[377]

Throughout much of the 1910 season, however, the Cubs would steal back the attention of the city's baseball fandom. Defeated in his quest for another world pool championship, Kling rejoined the Cubs in 1910. While Kling had fewer than three hundred at-bats for the season,[378] the Cubs again won 104 games in 1910, which this time was good for their fourth pennant, as they ended up 13 games ahead of second-place New York.

In 1910, the Cubs benefited from slugging a startling thirty-four home runs[379] and were pleasantly surprised by the quick development of rookie pitcher Len "King" Cole, who finished the season 20-4. The Cubs started slowly but went into first place for good on May 24. On July 11, the race was still close, as the Giants trailed the Cubs by only one and a half games. The Cubs beat the Giants that day in Chicago. It was the first of five straight defeats for the Giants and the first of nine losses in twelve games.[380]

Coincidentally (or maybe not), the next day, the Tinker-to-Evers-to Chance double-play combination became immortalized by *New York Mail* newspaperman Franklin P. Adams.[381] His column and verse that day was officially entitled "Baseball's Sad Lexicon," but it has become known over the years as "Tinker to Evers to Chance":

These are the saddest of possible words—
Tinker to Evers to Chance.
A trio of bear Cubs fleeter than birds—
Tinker to Evers to Chance.
Ruthlessly pricking our gonfalon bubble—
Making a Giant hit into a double—
Words that are weighty with nothing but trouble—
Tinker to Evers to Chance.[382]

What is not well known is that double plays were not then an official statistic. They did not become an official stat until 1919. No one knows for sure how many double plays the trio made. Sportswriter Charlie Segar determined that between 1906 and 1909, the three accounted for only fifty-six double plays scored 6-4-3 or 4-6-3. In fact, in the eight years they played together, neither Chance nor Evers ever led the league in double plays at their respective positions, and Tinker only once.[383]

The Giants' July slump, which coincided with the publication of the "Sad Lexicon," effectively finished them off for the season. By the end of August, the Cubs were leading the Pirates by 10 games and the Giants by 12, and they cruised to their fourth pennant in five years. The Cubs repeated their impressive feat of 1909, winning 104 games. This time, they captured the National League pennant as well.

Chapter 2

THE WORLD SERIES

The Cubs' opponent in the 1910 World Series was Connie Mack's Philadelphia A's. The opening two games would be played at Philadelphia's steel-and-concrete Shibe Park, built just a year before. In Game One, the Cubs' Orval Overall was not up to his usual standards and was roughed up by the A's. In the meantime, A's pitcher "Chief" Bender (so nicknamed because of his Native American heritage) held the Cubs to three hits in the Philadelphia victory.

While the Cubs were hardly dejected after one loss, history had not been kind to the loser of the opening game of each of the seven prior World Series. In all such cases, the winner of the first game won the series. Nonetheless, many Cubs players and fans were confident that another Chicago world title was inevitable. For example, after the Game One loss, Sol Hofman said: "That's about the least discouraging defeat we ever suffered. Of course, there isn't one of us wasn't sore about losing the first game, but there isn't one of us that doesn't believe we will take tomorrow's game and the next three after that."[384] Hofman then confidently predicted that the Cubs would bounce back and win four straight. After all, Chicago would have Mordecai Brown ready to pitch in Game Two, and Hofman was understandably confident.

While Hofman might have had cause for optimism, the results of Game Two would show that he did not have any psychic powers. In that game, the Cubs and Brown were manhandled, 9–3, by the A's. The Cubs were now down two games to none.

The two league champions traveled to Chicago and West Side Grounds for Game Three. The Cubs' train ride home was subdued, and when the train pulled into Union Station, a large contingent of fans was there to greet them—although not as large as one would have expected if the Cubs had won at least one game in Philadelphia and certainly not as boisterous. Gamblers who had originally put money on the Cubs were beginning to sense that this aging team could not compete with the younger A's.[385] Even for the most rabid Cubs fan, so accustomed to backing a perennial winner, doubt was beginning to creep in.

Game Three also went to the A's by another lopsided score, 12–5, putting the Cubs in a three-games-to-zero hole. Worse, in Game Three, Frank Chance became the first player ejected from a World Series game following his argument with future Hall of Fame umpire Tom Connolly. By now, the confidence and swagger that had characterized the mindset of Cubs fans had given way to doubt. As the days of the great Cubs dynasty appeared numbered, once-loyal fans were turning on their old heroes, and a *Tribune* article both chided Cubs fans for their "reproach" and offered little hope that the team would return to glory. "The disintegration of former greatness, whether in baseball or anything else, is pitiable. If the Cubs machine, our proud boast of four more years, is disintegrating, its members deserve sympathy, not reproach, as there are years of active diamond work near an end."[386] In hindsight, it seems ironic that Cubs fans back then would express "reproach" for their team merely because they were behind in the World Series, whereas Cubs fans over the next century or so would have given almost anything just to see their team in—even if losing—the World Series.

As the Peerless Leader would later reveal, the Cubs players had doubts of their own, which had apparently persisted throughout the season. After being removed as manager in 1912, Chance exploded in an interview with the press: "We haven't had a pitching staff for three years. Actually we used to laugh to ourselves to think we were up there fighting for the pennant and actually winning in 1910, when some of us realized we were a second division club."[387] Now they faced not only their own doubts but elimination in Game Four. Things weren't made any better by the fact that the A's Chief Bender, who had pitched so brilliantly in Game One, was ready to pitch Game Four and drive the final nail in the Cubs' World Series coffin.

The Cubs, however, would not pull up their tent and go home. In Game Four, with one out in the ninth inning and the Cubs trailing, Chance drove in the tying run, and Jimmy Sheckard drove in the winner in the tenth as the Cubs eventually scored a 4–3 victory. Sheckard, celebrating on his way to the clubhouse after his game-winning hit, was met about fifty feet from his destination by suddenly exuberant fans who carried him "shoulder-high" the rest of the way.[388] After the victory, former Cubs owner James A. Hart noted how those thousands of fans who had been so critical of the team during the last three losses suddenly, with one victory, had become rooters again. He added, "There is no doubt that the American baseball fan is the most forgiving or possibly the ficklest mortal in existence."[389]

Sheckard's game-winning hit would be the Cubs' last and only hurrah in the 1910 World Series. The A's mopped up in Game Five, claiming the world championship, four games to one. It would be the first of seven consecutive times—1910, 1918, 1929, 1932, 1935, 1938 and 1945—that the Cubs would go to the World Series but come away on the short end.

PART VIII

POST-1910

There was no need to inform us of the protocol involved.
We were from Chicago and knew all about cement.
—Groucho Marx, after leaving an imprint of his hand
in the cement at Grauman's Chinese Theater in Hollywood

Chapter 1

CHANGE

After 1910, the courses of the Cubs, semipro baseball and the city of Chicago began to change. The Cubs dynasty began to unravel. Charles Murphy never forgave Kling for abandoning the team in 1909 and traded him to the Braves in June 1911. In the meantime, Frank Chance, who had incurred hearing loss and agonizing headaches because of numerous beatings and brawls over the course of his career, was paying the price, losing his hearing in one ear and partially in the other. He developed blood clots in his brain from all of the beatings he took in his career.

With Sheckard and Kling gone and Chance disabled for much of the year, by the end of 1911, the Cubs' great run of four pennants and two world championships in five years had come to an end. The years immediately following would be no better.

By 1911, the wheels were also beginning to come off the cart of Chicago's semipro baseball scene. That year, Callahan left his semipro club and rejoined the White Sox, and semipro teams became less aggressive in recruiting major leaguers.[390] By then, the overall quality of Chicago's semipro teams began to decline. The top clubs returned to playing as independents, and the City League was no longer the major attraction it had once been. The number of semiprofessional teams in the city declined substantially.[391]

In Chicago city life, 1911 brought with it the decline of some of the icons of the Levee. Torchlight protests organized by reform advocates and religious leaders proclaimed their repugnance of the lawlessness of the Levee, insisting that gambling establishments and brothels be shuttered. The push by reformers influenced Mayor Carter Harrison to appoint commissions to investigate houses of prostitution throughout the city. The commissions concluded that there were more than twenty-seven million paid hook-ups per year in a city of just over two million people.

Just how prevalent the sex trade was in the city was illustrated when one commission appointed by the mayor interrogated a middle-aged, somewhat overweight prostitute. She told the commission that she would typically bring thirty men per night to her third-floor room. An appalled female commissioner exclaimed, "Why, that's terrible!" The prostitute, apparently in all seriousness, responded, "Yes, those stairs are killing me!"[392]

As a result of those investigative commissions, the Everleigh Club was raided. Mayor Harrison then ordered the Everleigh Club shut down,[393] and the sisters left town with over $1 million in cash, jewelry, stocks and bonds. In 1912, Harrison shut down the entire Levee District.

Later, of course, the onset of Prohibition in 1919 brought to the city a level of killing and violence that would make the brawling, corruption and vice of the twentieth century's first decade seem quaint and would further reinforce Chicago's reputation as a crime capital for generations.

Chapter 2

LEGACIES

By 1912, Chance was continuing to suffer headaches and dizziness throughout the season. The headaches were so bad that he had to forego playing in the field and instead managed solely from the bench. In midsummer in St. Louis, when the heat made his headaches unbearable, he had to leave the team and return to Chicago. He was even hospitalized and underwent brain surgery that year in New York.[394]

In his hospital room, Chance received a visit from Cubs owner Charles Murphy. The visit turned into a heated exchange between the two men over Murphy's releasing good players to save money. Not long afterward, Chance—unbelievably—was fired as both player and manager of the team. President Murphy defended his action by claiming that the team drank too much. Chance strongly denied those accusations.

Amazingly recovering from his brain injuries and his brain surgery, in 1913, Chance took over as manager of the New York Yankees, then also known as the Highlanders. At that time, before the arrival of Babe Ruth, they were a second-rate team. Chance spent the 1913 and 1914 seasons as player-manager for the hapless Yankees, resigning late in the 1914 season.

Ironically, Chance's move to the American League resulted in his being honored with a "Frank Chance Day" in Chicago—but not by the Cubs. Rather, the White Sox celebrated his incredible baseball career in the city. In March 1913, with the baseball schedule providing that Chance and his Highlanders would be visiting Comiskey Park to play the White Sox in mid-May, the city began making plans for a "Frank Chance Day." A blue-ribbon committee of who's who in Chicago, including Governor Edward F. Dunne, Mayor Carter Harrison, future baseball commissioner Kenesaw Mountain Landis, former mayor Fred Busse, entertainer George M. Cohan and "sausage king" Oscar N. Mayer, was appointed, and it organized a day of festivities on May 17, including a parade of 280 autos driving from the Board of Trade to Comiskey Park.[395]

At Comiskey Park that day, a party atmosphere prevailed. A huge crowd of approximately thirty-five thousand Chicagoans attended, many arriving as early as 8:00 a.m. While a band played during pregame ceremonies, Chance made his appearance on the field, and the crowd let out a boisterous cheer that drowned out the band. According to local news accounts, "From the instant Chance edged his way through the heavy fringe of spectators surrounding the field until the game was nearly over the great crowd rooted for Chance and for his team."[396]

Continuing pregame ceremonies, Chance approached home plate, led by Governor Dunne and Mayor Harrison. On reaching home plate, Chance was met by Sox manager Jimmy Callahan, and both managers were presented with elaborate floral arrangements by Dunne. Then Harrison presented Chance with the keys to the city.[397] Chance and his New Yorkers won the game, and the day provided a fitting tribute to one of Chicago's greatest sports figures and leaders.

Chance had been one of the builders, the player-manager and the best player of the last Cubs dynasty. That dynasty included the 1906 Cubs, whose 116 wins were the most of any Major League Baseball team of the twentieth century. Chance's Cubs won NL pennants in 1906, 1907, 1908 and 1910. More importantly, Chance's Cubs would win two world championships. He is the only manager (and a player-manager at that) of the twentieth century to win a world championship for the Cubs.

Chance moved back to California after his baseball career was over and died in 1924. He was elected to the National Baseball Hall of Fame in 1946, along with Joe Tinker and Johnny Evers.

////

For decades, Bathhouse Coughlin and Hinky Dink Kenna reaped the benefits from Chicago's First Ward citizens and establishments, although their influence was diminished in Al Capone's heyday. Together, they served as the ward's two aldermen until 1923, when only one alderman was permitted to serve. Coughlin was the ward's sole alderman from 1923 until his death in 1938. At Bathhouse's death, Hinky Dink succeeded him and served as First Ward alderman until his death in 1946.

Just as their two personalities were completely different, so were their respective funeral receptions. When he died, Coughlin was nearly penniless, but his funeral and procession were attended by thousands. The procession was led by Mayor Edward Kelly and a throng of the city's elite. A brass band accompanied the procession. The church was packed to overflowing for the funeral service.

Hinky Dink, in contrast to Bathhouse, left an estate of more than $1 million to heirs at his death. Compared to the funeral of Bathhouse, however, Hinky Dink's was a relative letdown. Attendees expected to see thousands at the funeral, but while some politicians showed up, the church wasn't filled to overflowing. Mayor Kelly didn't show; word was that he went to Boston to see a ball game. As his friends noted then about the usually withdrawn Kenna, "If you don't go to people's funerals, people won't go to yours." There was more postmortem disrespect for Kenna. His will provided that, of the $1 million being left to his heirs, $33,000 be used to build a mausoleum to house his remains. Kenna's heirs, however, spent only $85 for a tombstone and kept the remainder.

////

Daniel Burnham suffered from health problems in his later years, including the years he was developing plans for San Francisco and Chicago. Nonetheless, in 1910, he was appointed by President Taft as the first chairman of the National Commission on Fine Arts.[398] The award was one that Burnham cherished. When he passed away in 1912, he had an international reputation. He left a legacy of beauty and order, and President Taft called him "one of the foremost architects of the world."

PART IX

EPILOGUE

One thing you learned as a Cubs fan: when you bought your ticket,
you could bank on seeing the bottom of the ninth.
—Joe Garagiola, who played catcher for the dismal Cubs teams
of 1953 and 1954

In the century after the Cubs' 1908 world championship, the team would compile an overall record that could only generously be described as mediocre. "Bleak" would be a better word. Things got so bad for Cubs fans that Moe Drabowsky, who pitched for the team in the 1950s, took the field at Wrigley Field one Opening Day and saw a fan holding a sign: "Wait 'til Next Year!"

Many explanations have been offered over the years for the Cubs' dismal performance from 1908 to 2016. Those explanations range from the reasonable (the physical toll taken from playing day baseball in midsummer heat), to the bizarre (the curse of the billy goat, the 1969 curse of the black cat or the century-old Murphy curse). Some have argued that the Cubs simply have not had sufficient talent over the past century. The latter has an element of truth, of course, but is only partially true. For example, the 1962 and 1966 Cubs teams each featured four future Hall of Famers (Banks, Santo, Williams and Brock in 1962; Banks, Santo, Williams and Jenkins in 1966), but those teams had two of the most dismal seasons in Cubs history.

David Halberstam's book about a decades-long baseball friendship, *The Teammates*, revealed the thoughts of Red Sox second baseman Bobby Doerr on the New York Yankees' decades of success. Doerr believed that the Yankees had a "simple formula" for success in which, as part of the formula, a "great All-Star quality catcher" was "critical."[399] Indeed, over the decades, the Yankees featured a succession of great, All-Star, league-dominating catchers, including Bill Dickey, Yogi Berra, Elston Howard,

Thurman Munson and Jorge Posada, each of whom caught for at least two Yankee World Series champion teams.

Doerr's belief that great catchers were critical to the Yankees' success can be applied—to a lesser degree, of course—to Cubs history. Since 1900, the Cubs have had some very good, even All-Star, catchers——including Randy Hundley, Jody Davis, Steve Swisher and Wilson Contreras, among others— but arguably only two great, league-dominating catchers: Johnny Kling and Hall of Famer Gabby Hartnett.

In the twentieth century, the Cubs won ten National League pennants, and of those ten, eight featured league-dominating catchers Kling (whose Cubs teams won four pennants, in 1906, 1907, 1908 and 1910) or Hartnett (whose teams won another four pennants, in 1929, 1932, 1935 and 1938). Furthermore, the two pennant-winning years in the twentieth century without either Kling and Hartnett behind the plate were 1918 and 1945— two world war years of disruption when hundreds of major league players left the game to serve in the military and major league standings may have been skewed. In other words, history tells us that when, and only when, the Cubs have a great, league-dominating catcher like Kling (four pennants) or Hartnett (four pennants), multiple pennants result.

Finally, while it is conceded that the Cubs won their eleventh pennant, along with the World Series, in 2016 with no league-dominating catcher (Miguel Montero, David Ross and then rookie call-up Wilson Contreras handled the catching duties), there were no other—let alone multiple— pennants with those catchers, as there were with Kling and Hartnett.

If the Cubs ever hope to repeat their run of the invincible summers of 1906–10, they may need to build a team that emulates the same talent, toughness, smarts, reliance, imagination and swagger that were the hallmarks of the dynasty in the early 1900s. They may also consider doing whatever it takes to feature a great, league-dominating catcher. That would be a good place to start.

NOTES

Part I

1. Adam Selzer, *Chronicles of Old Chicago* (New York: Museyon, 2014), 18.
2. Ibid., 21, 22.
3. Reid Badger, *The Great American Fair: The Columbian Exposition* (Chicago: Nelson Hall, 1979), 31, 32.
4. Ibid., 32.
5. "The Great White-Red Stocking Game To-day," *Chicago Tribune*, September 7, 1870.
6. The History Channel: This Day in History, "Cincinnati Red Stockings Become First Professional Baseball Team," https://www.history.com.
7. "Great White-Red Stocking Game To-day," *Chicago Tribune*; "White above the Red," *Chicago Tribune*, September 8, 1870.
8. "White above the Red"; "The National Game: Some Reminiscences of the Late White-Red Stocking Contest," *Chicago Tribune*, September 9, 1870.
9. Ibid.
10. "The National Game: Three Thousand Citizens Welcome Home the White Stockings," *Chicago Tribune*, September 10, 1870.
11. Philip J. Lowry, *Green Cathedrals* (New York: Walker & Co., 2006), 47.

Part II

12. *Chicago Tribune* staff, *Chicago Days* (Chicago: Contemporary Books, 1997), 38; Badger, *Great American Fair*, 32.

13. *Chicago Tribune* staff, *Chicago Days*, 37.

14. Jerome Holtzman and George Vass, *The Chicago Cubs Encyclopedia* (Philadelphia: Temple University Press, 1997), 322.

15. Badger, *Great American Fair*, 32.

16. Ibid., 32.

17. "Speak Softly; Carry Big Stick; Says Roosevelt," *Chicago Tribune*, October 11, 1871, 1.

18. Gregg Lee Carter, "Baseball in Saint Louis, 1867–1875: An Historical Case Study in Civic Pride," *Bulletin of the Missouri Historical Society* 31, no. 4 (1976): 255, 260, quoting Wyatt Winton Belcher, *The Economic Rivalry between St. Louis and Chicago: 1850–1880* (New York: Columbia University Press, 1947).

19. Russell Lewis, "From Shock City to City Beautiful," *Chicago History Magazine* (Fall 2010): 14.

20. *Chicago Tribune* staff, *Chicago Days*, 46.

21. David McCullough, *Mornings on Horseback* (New York: Simon & Schuster, 2001), 296.

22. Badger, *Great American Fair*, 37.

23. Ibid., 37, 38.

24. Chicago History Museum, Newberry Library and Northwestern University, *Encyclopedia of Chicago: Creating the Plan*, accessed May 12, 2005, http://www.encyclopediachicagohistory.org.

25. *Chicago Tribune* staff, *Chicago Days*, 68, 69.

26. Larry Lester, Sammy J. Miller and Dick Clark, *Black Baseball in Chicago* (Charleston, SC: Arcadia Press, 2000), 9.

27. Daniel Okrent and Steve Wulf, *Baseball Anecdotes* (New York: Oxford University Press, 1989), 52.

28. Ibid.

29. Caitlin Murphy, *Crazy '08: How a Cast of Cranks, Boneheads, and Magnates Created the Greatest Year in Baseball History* (New York: HarperCollins, 2007), 47.

30. Lincoln Steffens, *The Shame of the Cities* (Mineola, NY: Dover, 1904), 163.

31. Badger, *Great American Fair*, 36.

32. Ibid.

33. Ibid.

34. Chicago Public Library, "Crime," http://chipublib.org/004chicago/1900/crime.html.
35. William T. Stead, *If Christ Came to Chicago* (Chicago: Laird and Lee, 1894), 183; see also Library of Congress, https://www.loc.gov/item/05030353.
36. Ibid.
37. Ibid.
38. Melissa Lafsky, "The Golden Age of Chicago Prostitution, A Q&A with Karen Abbott," *Freakonomics* (blog), August 1, 2007, http://freakonomics.blogs.nytimes.com.
39. Chicago Public Library, "Family Economics," http://www.chipublib.org.
40. Troy Taylor, "Haunted Chicago: Bathhouse John, Hinky Dink and Chicago's History of Graft and Corruption," American Hauntings, www.prairieghosts.com.
41. *Chicago Tribune* staff, *Chicago Days*, 78.
42. Chicago Public Library, "Crime."
43. National Park Service, "Roosevelt's Bar Fight," www.nps.gov, August 10, 2015.
44. "Speak Softly; Carry Big Stick; Says Roosevelt," *Chicago Tribune*, April 3, 1903, 1.
45. Selzer, *Chronicles of Old Chicago*, 96.
46. Taylor, "Haunted Chicago."
47. *Chicago Crime Scenes Project* (blog), "Alderman John Coughlin's Basement Bathhouse," February 24, 2009, https://chicagocrimescenes.blogspot.com.
48. Ibid.
49. Lloyd Wendt and Herman Kogan, *Lords of the Levee* (Evanston, IL: Northwestern University Press, 2005), 91.
50. Ibid.
51. Ibid., 76, 77.
52. "Blood in the First," *Chicago Tribune*, April 4, 1894, 1.
53. "How the Gang Ran the First Ward," *Chicago Tribune*, April 5, 1894, 2.
54. Wendt and Kogan, *Lords of the Levee*, 103.
55. "Blood in the First," *Chicago Tribune*.
56. Ibid.
57. Ibid.
58. Ibid.
59. Ibid.
60. Ibid.
61. Ibid.; Wendt and Kogan, *Lords of the Levee*, 104, 105.

62. "Blood in the First," *Chicago Tribune.*

63. *Chicago Crime Scenes Project* (blog), "Alderman John Coughlin's."

64. Selzer, *Chronicles of Old Chicago*, 91.

65. Taylor, "Haunted Chicago."

66. Ibid.

67. *Ann Arbor (MI) Argus*, "Chicago Aldermen Are Cute," December 17, 1897.

68. National Baseball Hall of Fame, "Frank Selee," https://baseballhall.org.

69. Sean D. Hamill, "Now They Know: Jimmy Slagle Played Here," *New York Times*, November 6, 2007.

70. Holtzman and Vass, *Chicago Cubs Encyclopedia*, 197.

71. Mark Stang, *Cubs Collection: 100 Years of Chicago Cubs Images* (Wilmington, OH: Orange Frazer Press, 2001), 14.

72. Gil Bogen, *Johnny Kling, A Baseball Biography* (Jefferson, NC: McFarland, 2006), 6.

73. Ibid., 5.

74. Eddie Gold and Art Ahrens, *The Golden Era Cubs: 1876–1940* (Los Angeles: Bonus Books, 1985), 49.

75. Peter Golenbock, *Wrigleyville: A Magical History Tour of the Chicago Cubs* (New York: St. Martin's Press, 1996), 97.

76. Bogen, *Johnny Kling*, 4.

77. Gold and Ahrens, *Golden Era Cubs*, 49.

78. National Baseball Hall of Fame, "Frank Chance," https://baseballhall.org.

79. Donald Honig, *The Chicago Cubs: An Illustrated History* (New York: Prentice Hall, 1991), 18.

80. Ibid., 20.

81. See, in general, David Kaplan, *The Plan: Epstein, Maddon, and the Audacious Blueprint for a Cubs Dynasty* (Chicago: Triumph Books, 2017).

82. James Crusinberry, "Joseph B. Tinker, Manager of Chicago, et al.," *Chicago Tribune*, April 4, 1915.

83. Ibid.

84. Will Leonard, "Tinker to Evers to Chance," *Chicago History Museum Magazine* (Fall 1970): 72.

85. *Chicago Tribune*, April 4, 1915, *supra.*

86. Ibid.

87. Gold and Ahrens, *Golden Era Cubs*, 55.

88. Robert Smith, *Heroes of Baseball* (Cleveland, OH: World Publishing, 1953), 185.

89. John Evers and Hugh Fullerton, *Touching Second: The Science of Baseball* (Chicago: Reilly & Britton, 1910), 64; Smith, *Heroes*, 185.

90. Gold and Ahrens, *Golden Era Cubs*, 51.

91. Leonard, "Tinker to Evers to Chance," 74.

92. Gold and Ahrens, *Golden Era Cubs*, 43.

93. Cindy Thomson, "Mordecai Brown," Society of American Baseball Research (hereafter SABR), https://sabr.org.

94. History of Cardinals, "Mordecai 'Three Fingers' Brown—Maybe Worst Cardinals Trade," https://www.historyofcardinals.com.

95. Stang, *Cubs Collection*, 18, 19.

96. Gold and Ahrens, *Golden Era Cubs*, 43.

97. Stang, *Cubs Collection*, 30.

98. "Beat New York," *Chicago Tribune*, April 9, 1905.

99. Cappy Gagnon, "Ed Reulbach," SABR.

100. Holtzman and Vass, *Chicago Cubs Encyclopedia*, 25.

101. Honig, *Chicago Cubs*, 19–20.

102. David Fleitz, "Frank Selee," SABR.

103. Stang, *Cubs Collection*, 8.

104. Ibid., 27.

105. Emil Rother and Art Ahrens, "History of the Chicago City Series," SABR.

106. Holtzman and Vass, *Chicago Cubs Encyclopedia*, 376.

107. Stang, *Cubs Collection*, 23.

108. Murphy, *Crazy '08*, 91.

109. "Play Doc White to Win," *Washington Post*, October 8, 1906.

110. Ibid.

111. Holtzman and Vass, *Chicago Cubs Encyclopedia*, 143.

Part III

112. Upton Sinclair, *The Jungle* (New York: Doubleday, 1906), 27, 28.

113. Ibid., 61; Doris Kearns Goodwin, *Bully Pulpit* (New York: Simon & Schuster, 2013), 459.

114. *Encyclopedia Britannica*, "Chicago," 8; Edmund Morris, *Theodore Rex* (New York: Random House, 2001), 435.

115. Morris, *Theodore Rex*, 465.

116. "Murphy Pleased with Players," *Chicago Tribune*, April 6, 1906.

117. Ibid.

118. Ibid.

119. Ibid.

120. "Fans Await Cry of 'Play Ball'," *Chicago Tribune*, April 8, 1906.

121. "The San Francisco Horror," *Chicago Tribune*, April 19, 1906.

122. "Frisco Refugees Tell of Terrors," *Chicago Tribune*, April 23, 1906.

123. "Stream of Gold Chicago's Reply," *Chicago Tribune*, April 21, 1906.

124. Don Doxsie, *Iowa Baseball Greats* (Jefferson, NC: McFarland, 2015), 14.

125. Thomas S. Hines, *Burnham of Chicago: Architect and Planner* (Chicago: University of Chicago Press, 1997), 191–92.

126. Carl Smith, *The Plan of Chicago* (Chicago: University of Chicago Press, 2006), 68.

127. Richard J. Roddewig, "Law as Hidden Architecture: Law, Politics and Implementation of the Burnham Plan Since 1909," *John Marshall Law Review*, 375, 376.

128. Smith, *Plan of Chicago*, 52.

129. Ibid., 66–67.

130. *Encyclopedia of Chicago*, "Plan of Chicago."

131. Smith, *Plan of Chicago*, 68, 69.

132. "Wahoo" Sam Crawford, as quoted in L. Ritter, *The Glory of Their Times* (Holtzman Press, 1966), 56.

133. *Chicago Tribune*, "Fans in Joyous Mood," May 20, 1906.

134. Fred Snodgrass, as quoted in Ritter, *Glory of Their Times*.

135. Larry Brunt, "Christy Mathewson: The First Face of Baseball," National Baseball Hall of Fame, https://baseballhall.org.

136. Holtzman and Vass, *Cubs Encyclopedia*, 26.

137. "Fans Think Flag Is Won," *Chicago Tribune*, July 22, 1906.

138. Bryan Soderholm-Difatte, "The 1906–10 Cubs: The Greatest Team in National League History," *Baseball Research Journal* (Spring 2011).

139. See Holtzman and Vass, *Cubs Encyclopedia*, 26.

140. Ibid.

141. James Doherty, "The Story of Bathhouse John," *Chicagology* (blog), https://chicagology.com.

142. Richard C. Lindberg, *The White Sox Encyclopedia* (Philadelphia: Temple University Press), 11.

143. Explore PA History, "Edward Walsh, circa 1911," https://explorepahistory.com.

144. Stuart Schimler, "Big Ed Walsh," SABR.

145. Ibid.

146. "Far from Diamond Sox Gain Crown, et al.," *Chicago Tribune*, October 4, 1906.

147. Ibid.

148. Hugh Fullerton, "Sox Join Cubs, Pennant Is Won," *Chicago Tribune*, October 4, 1906.

149. "Chicago Seized by a Baseball Frenzy," *Chicago Daily News*, October 9, 1906.

150. Charles Dryden, *Chicago Tribune*, "Horse Blanket Series: Dryden," October 9, 1906.

151. "Fans Are in Full Blast," *Chicago Daily News—Sporting Extra*, October 9, 1906.

152. Ibid.

153. "Baseball at a Climax," *Chicago Daily News*, October 9, 1906.

154. "Fans Are in Full Blast," *Chicago Daily News—Sporting Extra*.

155. Evers and Fullerton, *Touching Second*, 16, 17.

156. Ibid.

157. "Fans Are in Full Blast," *Chicago Daily News—Sporting Extra*.

158. Evers and Fullerton, *Touching Second*, 16, 17.

159. Hugh Fullerton, "Series Verifies Fullerton's Dope," *Chicago Tribune*, October 15, 1906.

160. Ibid.

161. "Jones Is Confident," *Washington Post*, October 4, 1906.

162. "Sox Win the First," *Washington Post*, October 10, 1906.

163. Ibid.

164. Lowry, *Green Cathedrals*, 49.

165. "Final Results—White Sox, 2; Cubs, 1," *Chicago Daily News—Sporting Extra*, October 9, 1906.

166. "Fans in Halls See Game," *Chicago Tribune*, October 10, 1906.

167. "Baseball at a Climax," *Chicago Daily News*, October 9, 1906.

168. Ibid.

169. Ritter, *Glory of Their Times*, 79.

170. "Final Results—White Sox, 2; Cubs, 1," *Chicago Daily News—Sporting Extra*.

171. "Sox Win the First," *Washington Post*.

172. Ibid.

173. Ibid.

174. "Sox Gain Victory in First Big Game," *Chicago Tribune*, October 10, 1906.

175. Ibid.

176. Lindberg, *White Sox Encyclopedia*, 11.

177. Bruce A. Rubenstein, *Chicago in the World Series, 1903–2005* (Jefferson, NC: McFarland, 2006), 7.

178. "Fans Are Loyal in Cold," *Chicago Daily News—Sporting Extra*, October 10, 1906.

179. "Nationals Win, 7–1 in Second Game," *Chicago Tribune*, October 11, 1906.
180. "Fans Are Loyal in Cold," *Chicago Daily News—Sporting Extra*.
181. "Notes for Fandom," *Washington Post*, October 11, 1906.
182. I.E. Sanborn, "Nationals Win 7–1 in Second Game," *Chicago Tribune*, October 11, 1906.
183. Golenbock, *Wrigleyville*, 122.
184. Charles Dryden, "Beaten by Nose…Players Annex Colds," *Chicago Tribune*, October 12, 1906.
185. I.E. Sanborn, "Rohe and Walsh Win for the Sox," *Chicago Tribune*, October 12, 1906.
186. Ibid.
187. Ibid.
188. Golenbock, *Wrigleyville*, 122.
189. "Rohe's Triple Wins," *Washington Post*, October 12, 1906.
190. I.E. Sanborn, "Rohe and Walsh Win for the Sox," *Chicago Tribune*, October 12, 1906.
191. "Notes of the Game," *Washington Post*, October 12, 1906.
192. "Alderman Martin Rides in Patrol Wagon," *Chicago Tribune*, October 12, 1906.
193. Ibid.
194. Ibid.
195. Ibid.
196. "Notes," *Washington Post*, October 13, 1906.
197. "Nationals Take Fourth Game, 1–0," *Chicago Tribune*, October 13, 1906.
198. "Notes of the Game," *Washington Post*, October 13, 1906.
199. Ibid.
200. Evers and Fullerton, *Touching Second*, 17.
201. "Sox Win 8–6," *Boston Daily*, October 14, 1906.
202. "Hats Off to the White Sox," *Boston Globe*, October 15, 1906.
203. Ibid.
204. "Sox Are Champions," *Washington Post*, October 15, 1906.
205. Charles Dryden, "Swift Kick Beats Spuds: Boot, Applied to Schulte," *Chicago Tribune*, October 15, 1906.
206. "Sox Are Champions," *Washington Post*.
207. "Hats Off to the White Sox," *Boston Globe*.
208. "Frantic Rooters Crowd the Field," *Chicago Tribune*, October 15, 1906.
209. "Hats Off to the White Sox," *Boston Globe*.
210. "Frantic Rooters Crowd the Field," *Chicago Tribune*.
211. Ibid.

212. Ibid.

213. Ibid.

214. Lindberg, *White Sox Encyclopedia*, 432.

215. "Frantic Rooters Crowd the Field," *Chicago Tribune*.

216. Ibid.

217. Ibid.

218. Baseball Almanac, "1906 World Series," www.baseball-almanac.com.

219. Ray Schmidt, "The Golden Age of Chicago Baseball," *Chicago History Magazine* (Winter 2000): 49.

220. *Encyclopedia of Chicago*, "Baseball"; Schmidt, "Golden Age," 52.

221. Schmidt, "Golden Age," 49.

222. Ibid., 52.

223. Ibid., 50.

224. Patrick Mallory, "The Game They All Played: Chicago Baseball, 1876–1906" (PhD diss., Loyola University, Chicago, 2013), https://ecommons.luc.edu.

225. Ibid.; Schmidt, "Golden Age," 50.

226. Schmidt, "Golden Age," 52.

227. Ibid.

228. *Chicago Tribune*, October 19, 1906 (lineups for the next day).

229. Ibid.

230. *Chicago Tribune*, October 22, 1906.

231. Schmidt, "Golden Age," 53.

232. *Chicago Tribune*, October 22, 1906.

233. Schmidt, "Golden Age," 53.

234. *Chicago Tribune*, "Plan Underway for City Beauty," December 13, 1906.

235. Smith, *Plan of Chicago*, 74.

Part IV

236. Soderholm-Difatte, "1906–10 Cubs."

237. Smith, *Heroes of Baseball*, 154.

238. Fred Snodgrass, as quoted in Ritter, *Glory of Their Times*.

239. Smith, *Heroes of Baseball*, 152.

240. Okrent and Wulf, *Baseball Anecdotes*, 46.

241. Hugh Fullerton, "Battles of the Ball Field," *Chicago Tribune*, July 22, 1906.

242. Ritter, *Glory of Their Times*, 123.

243. Chief Meyers, as quoted in Ritter, *Glory of Their Times*, 166.

244. Ritter, *Glory of Their Times*, 83.

245. Ibid., 14.

246. *New York Times*, "Umpires Attacked at Polo Grounds," May 22, 1907.

247. Ibid.

248. Ibid.

249. *New York Times*, June 9, 1907.

250. *Chicago Tribune*, October 6, 1907.

251. Charles Dryden, "Manager Chance Hurls Bottles," *Chicago Tribune*, July 9, 1907.

252. Ibid.

253. Ibid.

254. Charles Dryden, "Cubs Win; Chance Is Suspended," *Chicago Tribune*, July 10, 1907.

255. *Chicago Tribune*, "Black Hand after Chance?" August 18, 1907.

256. Ibid.

257. Ibid.; *Chicago Tribune*, "Cubs Nail Pennant to the Pole," September 24, 1907.

258. Gold and Ahrens, *Golden Era Cubs*, 49.

259. Charles Leehrsen, *Ty Cobb, A Terrible Beauty* (New York: Simon & Schuster, 2015), 25.

260. C. Paul Rogers III, "Hughie Jennings," SABR.

261. Ibid.

262. Holtzman and Vass, *Cubs Encyclopedia*, 354.

263. "Rejoicing Turns to Rioting," *Chicago Tribune*, October 7, 1907.

264. I.E. Sanborn, *Chicago Tribune*, "United Chicago Pulls for Cubs, October 6, 1907, C1.

265. "First Game Goes 12 Innings to Tie," *Chicago Tribune*, October 9, 1907.

266. Ibid.

267. I.E. Sanborn, "Cubs Win Again by Great Play," *Chicago Tribune*, October 12, 1907.

268. Ibid.

269. Ibid.

270. *Chicago Tribune*, "Streets Blocked by Cheering Fans," October 13, 1907, 2.

271. *New York Times*, "Cubs Win World's Baseball Honors," October 13, 1907.

272. Charles Dryden, "World Champions Play Exhibition Game," *Chicago Tribune*, October 14, 1907.

273. Holtzman and Vass, *Cubs Encyclopedia*, 28.

274. *Chicago Tribune*, "Charles Murphy Host at Banquet," December 12, 1907, 10.
275. Richard T. Griffin, "Sin Drenched Revels at the Infamous First Ward Ball," *Smithsonian Magazine* (November 1976): 52.
276. *Chicago Crime Scenes Project* (blog), "First Ward Ball," May 9, 2009, https://chicagocrimescenes.blogspot.com/2009/05/first-ward-ball.html.
277. Ibid.
278. Griffin, "Sin Drenched Revels at the Infamous First Ward Ball," 52.
279. "First Ward in Annual Orgy," *Chicago Tribune*, December 10, 1907.
280. Ibid.
281. "Sees Pagan Rome in First Ward Ball," *Chicago Tribune*, October 6, 1908.
282. "First Ward in Annual Orgy," *Chicago Tribune*.

Part V

283. "Notes of the Cubs," *Chicago Tribune*, June 9, 1908.
284. Murphy, *Crazy '08*, 92.
285. Don Jensen, "Jimmy Sheckard," SABR.
286. Gold and Ahrens, *Golden Era Cubs*, 51.
287. Soderholm-Difatte, "1906–10 Cubs."
288. Charles Dryden, "Cubs Twice Defeat Giants," *Chicago Tribune*, September 23, 1908, 8.
289. Murphy, *Crazy '08*, 190.
290. Ibid., 187.
291. Ibid., 190.
292. Ritter, *Glory of Their Times*, Bridwell section.
293. Don Doxsie, "Joe McGinnity" (sometimes spelled "McGinty"), SABR.
294. Dryden, "Game Ends in Tie, May Go to Cubs," *Chicago Tribune*, September 24, 1908.
295. See, e.g., Murphy, *Crazy '08*, 191.
296. Mordecai Brown, as told to *Chicago Tribune*, May 1, 1937; Joseph Tinker, as told to the *Chicago Tribune*, February 24, 1947; and John Evers, as told to John P. Carmichael in A.S. Barnes, *My Greatest Day in Baseball* (New York: Bantam Books, 1945), 39.
297. Evers and Fullerton, *Touching Second*, 187.
298. Dryden, "Game Ends in Tie," *Chicago Tribune*.
299. Ibid.
300. Ibid.

301. Ibid.

302. Holtzman and Vass, *Cubs Encyclopedia*, 189, 190.

303. Soderholm-Difatte, "1906–10 Cubs."

304. "Cubs Ordered to Play Off Tie Game," *Chicago Tribune*, October 7, 1908.

305. Harvey Woodruff, "Cubs Leave for New York to Play Deciding Game with Giants," *Chicago Tribune*, October 8, 1908.

306. "Cubs Rush on to Victory in the Battle of Today," *Chicago Tribune*, October 8, 1908.

307. Ibid.

308. *New York Sun*, as reported in *Chicago Tribune*, "Game Viewed by New York Eyes," October 9, 1908.

309. "The Cubs Win the Pennant," *New York Times*, October 9, 1908.

310. "Chicago Goes Wild Over Cubs Victory," *New York Times*, October 9, 1908.

311. "The Cubs Win the Pennant," *New York Times*.

312. Ibid.

313. "Sidelights on the Combat," *Chicago Tribune*, October 9, 1908.

314. "Game Viewed by New York Eyes," *New York Sun*, October 9, 1908.

315. Fred Snodgrass, as told in Ritter, *Glory of Their Times*, 100.

316. Ibid.

317. Retro Seasons, "Chicago Cubs Team Leaders 1908," https://www.retroseasons.com.

318. Art Ahrens, "Tinker v. Matty: A Study in Rivalry," SABR.

319. Christopher Mathewson, *Pitching in a Pinch* (New York: Grosset & Dunlap, 1912), 60.

320. Ibid.

321. "Chicago Goes Wild Over Cubs Victory," *New York Times*.

322. Mordecai Brown, as told in Holtzman and Vass, *Cubs Encyclopedia*, 3.

323. As told by M. Brown in *Chicago Tribune*, May 1, 1937.

324. Holtzman and Vass, *Cubs Encyclopedia*, 3.

325. *New York Evening Mail*, as reported in *Chicago Tribune*, "Gotham Game under Defeat," October 10, 1908.

326. "Chicago Goes Wild Over Cubs Victory," *New York Times*.

327. Historian Gabriel Schecter on the Cubs then, as quoted by Ed Sherman, *Chicago Tribune*, Oct 12, 2004.

328. I.E. Sanborn, "Cubs in Lead in World Series," *Chicago Tribune*, October 11, 1908; Holtzman and Vass, *Cubs Encyclopedia*, 355.

329. I.E. Sanborn, "Cubs Supreme in Baseball World," *Chicago Tribune*, October 15, 1908.

330. "Cubs Guests of Cohan," *Chicago Tribune*, October 16, 1908.

331. Mike Downey, "Curse on Cubs Originated with Murphy Snub," *Chicago Tribune*, February 8, 2007.

332. Ibid.

333. Griffin, "Sin Drenched Revels at the Infamous First Ward Ball," 7.

334. Ibid.

335. "Levee's Hordes Storm Coliseum," *Chicago Tribune*, December 15, 1908.

336. Curt Johnson and R. Craig Sautter, *Wicked City: From Kenna to Capone* (Chicago: DaCapo Press, 1998), 97; *Chicago Crime Scenes Project* (blog), "First Ward Ball," May 9, 2009, https://chicagocrimescenes.blogspot.com/2009/05/first-ward-ball.html.

337. "Levee's Hordes Storm Coliseum," *Chicago Tribune*, December 15, 1908.

338. Griffin, "Sin Drenched Revels at the Infamous First Ward Ball," 58.

339. *Chicago Examiner*, December 15, 1908; *Chicagology* (blog), "The First Ward Ball," http://chicagology.

340. Ibid.

341. Ibid.

342. *Chicago Crime Scenes Project*, "First Ward Ball."

343. Rick Kogan, "The First Ward Ball," *Chicago Tribune*, December 19, 2007.

Part VI

344. *Encyclopedia of Chicago*, "1909 Timeline."

345. "I'm Coming Back to Lead the Cubs," *Chicago Tribune*, February 7, 1909.

346. Ibid.

347. "John Kling Quits World Champs," *Chicago Tribune*, March 21, 1909.

348. Gold and Ahrens, *Golden Era Cubs*, 49.

349. "John Kling Quits World Champs," *Chicago Tribune*.

350. Holtzman and Vass, *Cubs Encyclopedia*, 29.

351. Gold and Ahrens, *Golden Era Cubs*, 48.

352. *Pittsburg Press*, January 5, 1910.

353. Lester, Miller and Clark, *Black Baseball in Chicago*, 7.

354. Linda Ziemer, "Chicago's Negro Leagues," *Chicago History Magazine* (Winter 1994–95): 44.

355. Ibid.

356. Lester, Miller and Clark, *Black Baseball in Chicago*, 23–25.

357. Harvey Woodruff, "Semi-Pros Enjoy Prosperous Year," *Chicago Tribune*, October 10, 1909.

358. R.W. Lardner, "Cubs Trim Giants in Final Game, 1–0," *Chicago Tribune*, October 23, 1909.

359. R.W. Lardner, "Cubs Rally Beats Leland Giants, 6–5," *Chicago Tribune*, October 22, 1909.

360. *Chicago History Today* (blog), "Gypsy Smith's March," October 18, 2017, https://chicagohistorytoday.wordpress.com.

361. Ibid.

362. Johnson and Sautter, *Wicked City*, 97.

363. Whet Moser, "The $12 Million Minute," *Chicago Magazine* (December 2014), https://www.chicagomag.com.

364. Brainy Quote, "Daniel Burnham," https://www.brainyquote.com.

365. Daniel Burnham and Edward Bennett, *Plan of Chicago* (Chicago: Commercial Club of Chicago, 1909), 188.

366. *Chicago Tribune* staff, *Chicago Days*, 94.

367. Lewis, "From Shock City to City Beautiful."

368. Dennis McLendon, *The Plan of Chicago: A Regional Legacy* (Chicago: Chicago Cartographics, 2008).

369. *Chicago Tribune* staff, *Chicago Days*, 95.

370. Thomas S. Hines, *Burnham of Chicago: Architect and Planner* (Chicago: University of Chicago Press, 2009), 246.

371. Ibid., 323.

372. Smith, *Plan of Chicago*, 83.

373. "Taft, a Loyal Fan, Sees Cubs Beaten," *Chicago Tribune*, September 17, 1909.

374. David Rapp, *Tinker to Evers to Chance: The Chicago Cubs and the Dawn of Modern America* (Chicago: University of Chicago Press, 2021), 241.

375. Smith, *Plan of Chicago*, 24.

376. *Chicago Tribune* staff, *Chicago Days*, 95.

Part VII

377. Lowrey, *Green Cathedrals*, 52, 53.

378. Holtzman and Vass, *Cubs Encyclopedia*, 30.

379. Ibid.

380. Soderholm-Difatte, "1906–10 Cubs."

381. Holtzman and Vass, *Cubs Encyclopedia*, 23; Soderholm-Difatte, "1906–1910 Cubs."

382. Honig, *Chicago Cubs*, 21.

383. Okrent and Wulf, *Baseball Anecdotes*, 51, 52.

384. Artie Hofman, "Game in Chicago to Turn the Tide," *Chicago Tribune*, October 19, 1910.

385. Ibid.; I.E. Sanborn, "Fans Greet Cubs on Arrival Home," *Chicago Tribune*, October 20, 1910.

386. Harvey Woodruff, "Are Cub Fans Willing to Be Known to the World as Quitters?," *Chicago Tribune*, October 22, 1910.

387. Harvey Woodruff, "Chance in Reply Lashes Cub Boss," *Chicago Tribune*, October 21, 1912.

388. James A. Hart, "Scoffers Again Cub Fans," *Chicago Tribune*, October 23, 1910.

389. Ibid.

Part VIII

390. Schmidt, "Golden Age," 57.

391. *Encyclopedia of Chicago*, "Baseball."

392. Johnson and Sautter, *Wicked City*, 8, 9.

393. Murphy, *Crazy '08*, 53.

394. Gregory Ryhal, "Frank Chance," SABR.

395. *Chicago Tribune*, March 30, 1913.

396. I.E. Sanborn, "Frank Chance Day Brings Out 35,000 but White Sox Win," *Chicago Tribune*, May 18, 1913.

397. Ibid.

398. Hines, *Burnham of Chicago*, 103.

Part IX

399. David Halberstam, *The Teammates* (New York: Hyperion, 2003), 166.

ABOUT THE AUTHOR

Gary D. Santella is a retired attorney who is a member of the Chicago History Museum and the Society of American Baseball Researchers (SABR). He is also a small-stake shareholder in the Atlanta Braves. He lives with his wife, Mary Kay, in a suburb of Chicago.

Visit us at
www.historypress.com